EDWARD BOND: THE PLAYWRIGHT SPEAKS

EDWARD BOND: THE PLAYWRIGHT SPEAKS

DAVID TUAILLON

Bloomsbury Methuen Drama
An imprint of Bloomsbury Publishing Plc

BLOOMSBURY
LONDON • NEW DELHI • NEW YORK • SYDNEY

Bloomsbury Methuen Drama
An imprint of Bloomsbury Publishing Plc
Imprint previously known as Methuen Drama

50 Bedford Square	1385 Broadway
London	New York
WC1B 3DP	NY 10018
UK	USA

www.bloomsbury.com

BLOOMSBURY, METHUEN DRAMA and the Diana logo are trademarks of Bloomsbury Publishing Plc

Originally published in the French language by Les Belles Lettres, Paris, France

© Les Belles Lettres, 2013

Published in the English language by Bloomsbury Methuen Drama in 2015

Les Belles Lettres have asserted their right under the Copyright, Designs and Patents Act, 1988, to be identified as author of this work.

All rights reserved. No part of this publication may be reproduced or transmitted in any form or by any means, electronic or mechanical, including photocopying, recording, or any information storage or retrieval system, without prior permission in writing from the publishers.

No responsibility for loss caused to any individual or organization acting on or refraining from action as a result of the material in this publication can be accepted by Bloomsbury or the author.

British Library Cataloguing-in-Publication Data
A catalogue record for this book is available from the British Library.

ISBN: HB: 978-1-4725-7014-7
PB: 978-1-4725-7006-2
ePDF: 978-1-4725-7011-6
epub: 978-1-4725-7010-9

Library of Congress Cataloging-in-Publication Data
A catalog record for this books is available from the Library of Congress

Typeset by Fakenham Prepress Solutions, Fakenham, Norfolk NR21 8NN
Printed and bound in India

CONTENTS

Talking to Edward Bond: Introduction by David Tuaillon 1

1 The one thing Shakespeare never does is despair 13
2 What is terrible about evil is not that it is banal but that it is domesticated 29
3 Language is an octopus with a million legs 49
4 In all these gaps there is the possibility of freedom 71
5 Truth can be very ugly but the desire for truth is always beautiful 91
6 Objects are people 111
7 The kitchen table and the edge of the universe 131
8 Reality doesn't become practical until it tells you its meaning 155
9 Nobody knows how to deal with innocence 177

Epilogue: The Stage is *Us* 199

TALKING TO EDWARD BOND: INTRODUCTION BY DAVID TUAILLON

The house is of rather modest dimensions and hides itself in the middle of a birch wood, somewhere in Cambridgeshire, in the most peaceful idea one can have of countryside; although it is deceptive, because there it seems that everything changes so that nothing changes – or is it the other way round? At one end of the single road that runs through the wood, you reach one of the densest concentrations of knowledge in the world, the huge complex of Cambridge University in its old-fashioned gothic buildings; at the other end begin the Fens, this undetermined and pre-history zone, where the land has not quite managed to take over the sea yet. People during the Neolithic Age left traces there; so did the Romans and the Templars too. Nearby is Fleam Dyke, that beaten-earth wall erected by the Saxons to protect themselves from the Britons during the chaos of the Dark Ages that followed the Roman retreat, which today resembles a giant molehill trail heading through the fields. In close proximity are several USAF air bases that housed NATO's nuclear bombers during the Cold War, once on the front line of the great peace movement of the 1980s, now nothing more than waste ground scattered with concrete ruins.

This is where Edward Bond took up residence in the early 1970s, when the success of his first plays allowed him the luxury of living away from London's turmoil – as well as contriving a homecoming to what had been the territory of his childhood. The neighbours used to call him 'the last man of the village'. He didn't stay that for long, though: first because he was soon joined by Elisabeth, a woman who came from deep within the continent to share his life and has done so ever since – and who now seems like a penates of the house; and second, because since his arrival, the two hamlets (the 'great' and the 'little') between which the house stands have been heavily gentrified into residential suburbs, quite affluent and without any history save the delusional new foundation that comes with money, so that even the most ancient farms with their immaculate whitewashed walls and impeccably combed thatches have become too iconic to be genuine any more.

During these more than forty years, the house has let itself be swallowed up by the vegetation of its large and lush garden. The garden is also home to a small, unexpected and inert community of statues, presents from friend-artists or improbable antiques rescued from here and there; too askew, mutilated or consumed by the greenery to be ostentatious, but seeming instead to sleep peacefully there, between the bushes and the copses, like some forgotten archaeology. They cohabit with a multitude of birds of all kinds, among them peacocks. Yes, real peacocks – most likely escaped from one of those outrageously wealthy residences that surround the nearby Newmarket racecourse and now established in new headquarters on their own authority. With their sliding and silent walk, like cautious skaters, their sudden squawking which always sounds a bit ironic, or their unexpected appearance, both majestic and grotesque, between the trees or in the frame of a window, they give this place the final touch of its singularly unreal and somewhat phlegmatic atmosphere.

As soon as you enter the house, you realize immediately that it is the life of its two inhabitants materialized – including its slightly shambolic air. On the first floor, half-dedicated to work, next to the library and its phenomenal disorder, a writing study nestles, saturated with books, papers and pictures but completely open to the light and foliage of the garden. The white and abstract brightness bathing the room, as well as the dominating thick silence troubled only by the haphazard calls of peacocks, emphasizes the palpable sense you feel here of being isolated from the world. And it is in this narrow room, warmly padded by the mute life of this still nature that isolates it from any violence or vulgarity outside, the core of this infinitely peaceful environment, with its slow and quiet country rhythm, that, day in day out, after he has fec the birds, Edward Bond – a large mug of white coffee in his hand – sits and writes down with urgency the inferno of our times.

Such is the spirit of the place, the *site*, in which most of the interviews you are about to read took place.

INTRODUCTION BY DAVID TUAILLON

   This paradoxical discrepancy between his drive to write about the world and his physical retirement from it deep inside a house sheltered beneath a magnificent, remote, ageless countryside also unwillingly mirrors Bond's actual situation in our present theatre. This is characterized by an extreme involvement in playwriting as well as by an intense exploration of what drama is and can be today, although he has physically kept away from the main stages for decades.
   Bond is today both unanimously celebrated as 'one of the greatest living playwrights' and ignored in his practical work, to the point that one has to wonder what it is exactly that keeps the media continuing to use this phrase that is inevitably associated with him. Except for one thing. As anyone googling his name would quickly discover, Edward Bond is the (in)famous author of Saved, the worldwide iconic and scandalous play of the late 1960s[1] which in the United Kingdom contributed to the final stroke that defeated theatre censorship[2] (Bond's subsequent play, Early Morning, actually holds the arguable distinction of having been the last play banned in toto in Britain), a historic fifty-year landmark that the publication of this book is intended to celebrate.
   Such a massive momentum that granted his work huge visibility and presence for years in virtually any field of performing arts,[3] as well as his close and lasting acquaintances with the most important institutions of British theatre during the heyday of each – the Royal Court from 1965 to 1975, the Royal Shakespeare Company from 1977 to 1985 and the National Theatre from 1978 to 1982 – have deeply inscribed Bond's name in the history of British drama, and specifically during what will probably come to be seen as its highlight in the twentieth century.[4] But as a counterpart, in the public's mind this tends to limit his work to that specific period, obscuring the fact that it has genuinely and practically continued to develop for fifty years. Bond has indeed written, published, seen staged (and on occasions directed himself[5]) no less than fifty-two plays since 1962, half of them after 1990, which is an awful lot more than the single Saved, itself much more than just a banned play of the 1960s.
   Admittedly, Bond's plays can't find their way to the English stage anymore since quite a long time. Certainly they are regularly published,[6] but one would look in vain for opportunities in Britain in the last, say, two decades to see the *current* work[7] of this *dramatist* (rather than, as relevant as they may still be, plays from forty or fifty

years ago) as it should be seen – that is, performed on a stage, supported by decent production conditions – to say nothing of the minimum care for the plays' genuine purpose, as bitterly claimed by their author.

The turning of the tide in cultural fashion is not the only thing to blame for this unbalanced perception. It also stems from the fact that Bond himself chose to desert the arena during the 1980s. Increasingly dissatisfied with the treatment of his plays by actors and directors and unable to impose himself as the director of his own plays, after quitting the disastrous rehearsals of his *War Plays* at the RSC in 1985 Bond literally turned his back on actual drama practice in his own country and, apart from rare and always frustrating exceptions, stayed away from the prestigious theatrical institutions where his work had flourished until then.[8] Bond's relationship with theatrical life in Britain has since been a story of constant misunderstanding and frustration on the part of all: professionals, critics, audiences, the writer himself. As he once put it, the whole ethos of theatre has changed since he entered it – which, after all, in the run of decades, is nothing but natural – but so has his own ethos, and they haven't followed the same direction, so the gap has grown unfathomably wider.

Since then, Bond has been mainly working with community theatre, students or modest companies (mostly reviving *Saved*) and drama teachers.[9] His main lasting and happy working relationship for the last twenty years has been with the Birmingham-based theatre-in-education company Big Brum, whose director Chris Cooper (and his predecessor, the late Geoff Gillham) has commissioned, produced and toured in classrooms ten new plays of his for young people. Bond's work has also recently experienced new and significant exposure in an important theatre in London, when Sean Holmes, the new head of the Lyric Theatre Hammersmith, staged two of his plays, involving Bond in the rehearsal process and subsequently offering him the opportunity to direct two of his more recent ones himself.[10] This case has, so far, remained unique.

Abroad, away from this polemical context, interest in Bond's plays, after an impressive peak following their discovery in the early 1970s, has also declined, but the plays have never completely disappeared from sight either. It would be tedious to list the various situations of Bond's work according to each country – which is also dependent on specific conditions and cultural contexts – and it is misleading to generalize, but we can see that here and there, the significance of Bond's work is regularly re-evaluated in the light of the revival of an old play or the production of a new one. One recent example, for instance, is Italy, where, following a celebrated production of *In the Company of Men* by Luca Ronconi in 2010, the Teatro di Roma is dedicating a specific programme to Bond's work around a new production of *Lear*.[11] In the German-speaking area, the translation and production of Bond's plays slowed down but never stopped, and in fact few of his later plays remain unknown there, though they are only modestly present on the official Berlin stages in a cultural context admittedly dominated by post-dramatic aesthetics, into which Bond's plays hardly fit. Over time, every year there have been one or more plays by Edward Bond on somewhere in the world, mostly but not exclusively in Europe, and he is still often invited overseas to support them. In particular, his recent plays for young people, *The Children* and *Have I None*, are international successes. Bond also constantly receives letters from students all over the world, including recently from Iraq and China, evidencing a wide interest in his work that exceeds any context of actual productions.

But nowhere else have the plays of Bond gained the status they hold in France. France demonstrated a late but strong interest in Bond's work in the early 1970s, mainly through controversial productions by two major French directors,[12] but it then had to wait until the early 1990s to get real lasting and significant attention. This was partly because, in this country where art is so organically politicized, Bond's scripts met the French stage's need for the kind of renewed political statements which it had steered clear of during the 1980s – a decade more focused on brilliance – and in the depressed context of the fall of communist regimes in Europe. This resurgence of interest in Bond's work happened thanks to the director Alain Françon who, especially in his role as director of the Théâtre national de la Colline (the main French stage dedicated to contemporary drama) for twelve years, kept offering great productions of Bond's new plays, sometimes against all odds and to actively reinforce his ideas on drama.[13] His production of *The War Plays*, an epic seven-hour open-air production at the Festival d'Avignon, met with enormous success and became a landmark in French theatre itself – to such an extent that Bond's name in France would definitely remain associated with those plays more than with

Saved, as it is everywhere else in the world. Since he's been seeing it, Bond has been very supportive of Françon's work and he subsequently wrote for him and his actors a series of plays he has since gathered under the label *Paris Pentad*.[14]

These productions truly introduced Bond to French audiences and made him the prominent and iconic dramatist he has been in this country ever since; the impulse for this book, initiated by a French researcher and first published for a French readership, significantly reflects this situation. As a result, but thanks also to the translation of Bond's theoretical work mainly conducted by the academic Jérôme Hankins, himself a director who also introduced in France Bond's plays for young audiences,[15] two-thirds of Bond's plays have already been staged in France and most of them are now available in translation. France, then, has built its own history with Bond's drama that is completely unconcerned with the situation in his homeland.

The central position that Bond occupies in France appears to be the direct opposite of his situation on the other side of the Channel, where his plays are kept in the margins of theatre life whereas his history remains at its core. After he parted with the official stage Bond did not stop working, neither did he lose his presence. He certainly did not disappear, nor has he been forgotten in the British theatrical landscape – as have many of his contemporaries who were similarly confronted with its changed ethos. He remains a broadly well-known figure, enjoys general regard, and is, as I already mentioned, repeatedly described as 'one of the greatest living dramatists'. New generations of upcoming playwrights and theatre-makers constantly claim to be inspired by his work – and one can see his influence in the work of Sarah Kane or Mark Ravenhill,[16] two well-known examples among others.

In fact, the paradox is that Bond is certainly known and recognized as the figurehead of an uncompromising drama, but, in the absence of his plays, as its spokesperson rather than in practice. Such ambivalence among the public also stems from Bond's own attitude. As a matter of fact, when he speaks publicly or is interviewed, instead of mentioning his own plays specifically, he always prefers to express, with a tireless profusion, the state of his fundamental and sometimes very abstract thoughts on the necessity for drama, its basis, its means, its possibilities – that is, to present the aims and objectives of his playwriting. Consequently, his real activity as a playwright is less known and commented on for its own sake than his statements, notoriously radical and attacking, about the present state of drama and the audacious perspectives he keeps ascribing it. And those perspectives are so impressive that Edward Bond as a writer is today more acknowledged, quoted, appreciated or criticized as an implacable preacher with clear-cut and provocative assertions, and the intimidating shadow cast by this figure contributes further to the concealment of his actual, proper dramatic work.

Hence a certain degree of misunderstanding and perplexity obliterates the debates and the reflexions by maintaining vain controversies and conflicts of standards in principle, which lazily insist on reducing Bond's thought to large views – ones that are not necessarily his – and seeing his plays, in spite of their immense effort of preciseness, as large gestures, as declarative as they are vague. Such conditions, too, prevent a reading of the plays for what they actually are and too often even discourage theatregoers and practitioners.

The whole purpose of this book, then, was to try to solve this frustrating situation by restoring the reality of Edward Bond's act of writing drama in order to allow his plays to speak, as it were, for themselves. This involved a journey away from the self-indulgent platitudes of theatrical circles back to the day-to-day work table of the writer – in other words, prior to any formalized discourse, to what happens in this long, quiet room that stretches between the garden and the library, at the end of this country house, inside the actual writing studio itself where most of these interviews took place.

In so doing, I was only replicating the private experience of numerous directors, dramatists and translators before me, who came – and still come – from the entire world to visit him prior to a production of one of his plays. In such a situation, Edward Bond demonstrates with simplicity – even sometimes with a certain levity – the ability to literally open up his plays; to unveil, in the most practical and concrete way, their construction, their movement and their issues, thereby revealing the density, the precision and the extraordinary consistency of his playwriting. Suddenly free from the common places into which his plays are usually tried to be forced, a new field of possibilities that seem quite new for drama opens up.

We can also then discover that this drama, so easily dismissed as recondite and domineering, is actually the product of a true listening to the dynamic and contradictory plurality of human beings and of an intense questioning which Bond intends, from the start, to provoke and keep alive in the spectator's mind. It also reveals a discourse in search of questions more than solutions, carried by a desire for truth and life which has little to do with denouncing and despondency, a poetics resting more on oddity than on shock – a dynamic which is not without humour or pleasure. Above all, it demonstrates a science of drama composition unique in its awareness of how signs work and articulate, in its grasp of the situation in all its tensions and contrasts, in its mastery of a scenic strategy of approach and suggestion to an audience based on a skilful organization of reason and imagination; and finally, in spite of the depth of the thought that produced it, unique in its sense of simplicity and pragmatism.

It is precisely in this dramatic material, incredibly fastidious, prolific and generous – though one has to learn to comprehend it and dig into it – that the true strength and vitality of Edward Bond's dramatic art lies. Far from setting up an authoritarian pressure, it aims to spur the insight of the interpreter's imagination and offers it a firm ground which really is a matchless invitation to creativity. This is what our interviews wished to bring to light, by foregrounding the plays themselves more than their theoretical frame and intentionally targeting those who would intend to practise this drama.

The interviews, amounting to almost a hundred hours, were carried out during winter and spring 2010/11 and worked on (that is, recomposed and re-edited and sometimes completed by assertions from other sources in order to form a reasoned and coherent whole) until early summer 2012. These two years were rich in events and news in the United Kingdom (the return to government of the Conservative Party, urban uprisings, the end of Rupert Murdoch's impunity, various royal self-congratulations) and beyond (popular revolutions in Tunisia, Egypt, Libya, Syria, the threefold catastrophe of 9 March 2011 in Japan, extreme impoverishment of Greece, rampant extension of the economic crisis in Europe, proliferation after the Spanish *Indignados* of the *Occupy* movements, etc.), as well as in Edward Bond's personal life, since it coincided with his first opportunity in years – mentioned above – to become involved in several productions of his plays in London. Even though we willingly toned down most of the direct references to these events in order to avoid limiting the material, such context remained present to us, in various respects, during our conversations, and it is probably useful for the reader to bear this in mind somehow while reading. Because Edward Bond didn't flee to the far corner of East Anglia to avoid the world but, on the contrary, so that he could listen to it better. Now it's our turn to listen to it with him.

David Tuaillon
August 2012 and November 2014

Notes

1. After its premiere at the Royal Court Theatre, London on 3 November 1965, directed by William Gaskill, *Saved* had no less than seventy-four productions worldwide between 1966 and 1974 (seventeen for the sole year 1968, whereas the play, ironically, was still banned in Britain), including countries such as Argentina, Yugoslavia, New Zealand and Israel, and more than twenty productions in West Germany alone (M. Hay and P. Roberts, *Edward Bond: A Companion to the Plays*, London: TQ Publications, 1978, pp. 79–84).

2. For a detailed account of this historic event see: http://www.theguardian.com/stage/2003/apr/23/theatre.samanthaellis

3. During the period from the late 1960s to the mid-1970s, in addition to his numerous plays Bond was commissioned for translations and adaptations, screenplays for TV and cinema, and librettos for opera and ballet. To take the year 1976 as one example (see M. Hay and P. Roberts, *Bond: A Study of His Plays*, London: Eyre Methuen, 1980, pp. 20, 216–37), Bond had on in London one new play (Royal Court, *The Fool*) and a revival (Royal Shakespeare Company, *Bingo*), plus two shorter plays offered to activist fringe companies (Gay Sweatshop, *Stone*; Almost-Free-Theatre, *A-A-America*), plus a commissioned adaptation of Webster's *The White Devil* for a trendy production at the National Theatre (by Michael Lindsay-Hogg, known as the director of *Let It Be* and *The Rolling Stones Rock and Roll Circus*) and an opera for which he wrote the libretto at the Royal Opera House, Covent Garden, Hans Werner Henze's *We Come to the River* (the same composer he was working with that same year on a ballet for William Forsythe, a project which never came to fruition).

4. See the comprehensive list of Bond's plays, their date and place of first production at the end of this book.

5. On Bond directing his own plays, see Ian Stuart's seminal study: *Politics in Performance: The Production Work of Edward Bond, 1978–1990*, New York: Peter Lang Publishing, 1996.

6   Bond's *Plays* reached volume 9 at Methuen in 2011, a record.

7   In that respect we can rule out the recent well-advertised production of *The Sea* (1972), directed by Jonathan Kent, premiered in January 2008 at the Theatre Royal Haymarket, and *Bingo* (1973), directed by Angus Jackson, premiered in April 2010 at the Chichester Festival Theatre, with which Bond strongly disagreed anyway.

8   For evidence (or, at least, Bond's point of view on this), see especially the second volume of his collected *Letters*, Ian Stuart (ed.), Luxemburg: Harwood Academic Publisher, 1995. The polemics with the English institutional stage are still vivid more than twenty-five years later, as can be seen in this late interview: http://www.theguardian.com/stage/2008/jan/03/theatre and the response it provoked: http://www.theguardian.com/stage/2008/jan/09/theatre2

9   See D. Davis (ed.), *Edward Bond and the Dramatic Child, Edward Bond's Plays for Young People*, London: Trentham Books, 2005.

10 *Saved* opened on 13 October 2011, *Have I None* on 19 April 2012, directed by Sean Holmes; *Chair* and *The Under Room*, directed by Edward Bond, opened the same day. It should be pointed out that this was preceded in autumn 2010 by an effort from the Cock Tavern, a pub in Kilburn, London with a 20-seat theatre upstairs, to produced no less than six of Bond's plays, one for each decade of his work including a new one: *Olly's Prison,* 14 September; *The Pope's Wedding,* 19 September; *The Under Room,* 5 October; *Red, Black and Ignorant,* 31 October; *The Fool*, 10 October, and an unfinished new play about Medea entitled *There Will Be More*, 26 October, the last two directed by Bond himself. The restricted size of the venue, though, limited the impact of this bold initiative.

11 *La Compania degli uomini*, Piccolo Teatro di Milano, 11 January 2010; *Lear*, directed by Lisa Ferlazzo Natoli, October 2015

12 *Sauvé*, directed by Claude Régy, TNP, Palais de Chaillot, Paris, 7 January 1972; *Lear*, directed by Patrice Chéreau, TNP, Villeurbanne, 8 April 1975.

13 At the Théâtre national de la Colline, Paris: *Café* (*Coffee*), 12 May 2000; *Le Crime du xxie siècle* (*The Crime of the 21st Century*), 9 January 2001; *Si ce n'est toi* (*Have I None*), 12 September 2003. At the Festival d'Avignon: *Pièces de guerre* (*The War Plays*), 17 July 1994; *Naître* (*Born*), 10 July 2006; *Chaise* (*Chair*), 18 July 2006. Also: *La Compagnie des hommes* (*In the Company of Men*), Paris, Théâtre de la ville, 29 September 1992; *Les Gens* (*People*), Théâtre Gérard Philipe, Saint-Denis, 13 January 2014. All of these were French premieres and the last four world premieres.

14 Due to the changing of labels as the series grew in number, it is worth stating that these are officially *Coffee, The Crime of the 21st Century,*

Born, *People* and *Innocence*. Only the latter three were actually written for Françon, but they were the result of Bond seeing his productions of the first two. The last one remains unproduced so far.

15   *Les Enfants*, Studio-Théâtre, Alfortville, 15 June 2002; *Le Numéro d'équilibre*, Festival d'Avignon, 10 July 2006; *La Flûte*, Théâtre des deux rives, Rouen, 4 April 2011.

16   See Ravenhill's warm accolade to Bond's work: http://www.theguardian.com/stage/2006/sep/09/theatre.stage

1
THE ONE THING SHAKESPEARE NEVER DOES IS DESPAIR

Telling very complicated things in a simple way / It is natural to write about violence / A sense of the apocalyptic: a childhood in the ruins / The human has become unfathomable / Poetry is only possible now if it belongs to drama / The most human character is Macbeth / Facing the ghosts / *Bingo*: allowing Shakespeare to criticize himself / White snow as a sheet of paper.

You have been writing since the early 1960s and you have now some fifty plays in store, including short and long plays, radio and TV plays, libretti for opera and ballet. How do you relate to this huge collection of dramatic works, some of which were written decades ago?

I am interested in what I am currently writing. I look at the earlier plays only when I have to – because they are being re-staged or I have to check them for reprinting. I have a very practical way of looking at them. My friend Chris Cooper, who directs the Big Brum TiE company, says I talk about my plays as if they were things or pets, as if I were going next door to rearrange things or give them a biscuit.

When I talk about my plays it sounds complicated, but drama is for me a way of telling very complicated things in a simple way because it tells them in an all-round way intellectually and physically. It is difficult to explain and it is difficult to obtain it in rehearsals – but it is not difficult for the audience in performance. They must know exactly what they are being shown so they can know how to interpret it and understand what it means. If they don't like what they are seeing that is another matter. Drama allows you to see things differently. If you begin to explain on the stage what you are doing, nothing happens. It is like giving a seventh sense to the audience. They just have to watch. It is very simple, but like every simple thing, once you start explaining everything becomes complicated. Isaac Newton used to write very complicated books (fortunately nobody had to act them) but they were actually explaining very small details. His friends worried about him because he wouldn't sleep enough, or eat properly and neglected himself to keep working ceaselessly. So one day they took him out to watch a tennis match. Newton was very interested but at the end, when his friends asked him who won, he couldn't say. All his attention was caught because when the players were hitting the ball, he noticed that it was … and then he started drawing a curve on the path because the ball wasn't describing the trajectory it would normally be thought it should. What he saw was not what the other people thought they saw. Well, that is what we have to do with the audience: make them notice what they wouldn't notice before. I want them to become specialists of themselves.

From the point of view of the writer, what has been changing from the 1960s until now?

When I started to write my plays it was still the aftermath of the Second World War, so we in the West knew what happens when things go really wrong. It reached its climax in Hiroshima and Auschwitz. We had this great crisis behind us which fuelled our writings. We could write out of our knowledge and say things have to change because what had happened was unbearable. It was natural for me to write about violence because I was conscious that the way we were living, the sort of politics and economy we had, was leading to disaster. What is happening now is that the crises are ahead of us. The great disasters have not yet occurred – and the young writers are not allowed to write about that.

You wrote it was 'natural' for you to write about violence as a comment on Saved, *your first play to be really noticed, in 1965. It was harshly attacked for its violence by the critics and censored under the responsibility of the Lord Chamberlain. The play remained banned for several years but opened a public debate that led to the abolition of censorship in Britain.*

At the time I was angry that the cultural elite and the critics had simply decided what was acceptable and what wasn't. I was outraged when the script of *Saved* came back from the Lord Chamberlain, literally marked with a blue pencil to show what his Lordship wouldn't allow! Finally driving censorship out of English theatre made it possible for us to have serious theatre, in the sense that the Greeks had: a theatre which can help us to understand ourselves, and to rule, order, govern our society in better ways, and to make it more free. That is what I thought would be the commitment of drama. I don't think that theatres can directly change society or usurp the role of political organization and representation, or replace people talking to each other in assemblies. Drama cannot replace politics but there would be no adequate politics without drama. That is the lesson I take from Athens. When Athens as a society became conscious that it was destroying itself and collapsing, this became the themes of its great dramatists. The Athenians were living in dangerous times so they needed drama to help them understand what was happening to them. It seems to be the opposite for us: we think we live in a time of prosperity and bounty, capitalism is creative and inventive and is, for the time being, convinced that it is able to solve all its problems and so it has made drama totally unserious and trivial.

What do you think has happened that led to this situation?

I said 'no' to censorship but since then capitalism has said 'yes' to the bank account. Drama has been turned into a commercial product that could be sold and it has lost its ability to actually be a political part of society and instead has become part of the marketplace. That emptied drama of all responsible content and made it un-political. At the most it becomes journalism. But it does not deal with its fundamental problems, which are the relationship between the self and society and how one creates the other.

Your plays are well known for dealing with wars and conflicts – and it is true that almost all of them deal with these things in one way or another. You have a direct experience of war yourself since you were a child in wartime, you lived in London during the Blitz.

Yes, this the modern citizen's terror of being in the middle of battles. Each time you hear a bomb fall (and they were falling in series) you say to yourself: 'This bomb must hit me, it's coming here.' Not: 'Is it going to kill me?' but: 'It is so close and its noise so intense, it must kill me.' Then there was the rocket-war with the V1s, first, which were crotchety and somehow stupid like wheelchairs racketing along the sky but soon afterwards there were the V2s which were real silent menaces, ghosts clad in steel – they exploded with a great hollow thump as they struck the earth as if they were knocking on a door and it opened. I remember very clearly the day the war ended: Churchill was on the radio, probably in the afternoon, saying: 'The Fascist beast has been kicked, driven to its lair' or something like that, and the little voice in me which used to say: 'This bomb will drop on you now', told me: 'So you will live.' I can still hear it. It sounds calm but a bit surprised. We were not in the worst-bombed places but the air battles were over London everywhere and bomb sites were dotted round the streets. From my front door I would see a house that had been bombed during the night; when I walked out there were always gaps where buildings had fallen, ruins with their sordid beauty: the houses with sides sheared away showing sagging floors still bearing some of the furniture, showing the different wallpapers in the different rooms and holes where the floor beams and stairs had been or fireplaces on the walls high up in space – for some reason I can remember especially a pink room and above it an acid light green room and a white section to the side, probably part of a stairwell – like a Matisse painting. And everywhere this smell of dust dust dust.

We often meet in your plays these sets and landscapes of ruins and wastelands with people trying to survive in them.

These ruins remained for some years afterwards and we were used to seeing them. So they became for me not a place of destruction but of survival and hope: this is where I survived. So there wouldn't be any more troubles. If you want an instance to figure this out, the last

THE ONE THING SHAKESPEARE NEVER DOES IS DESPAIR

scene of my play *Coffee*, which is set in a house in a bombed city, is an exact mental photograph of the world I was a schoolboy in. In the play I added the image of the dead body found in the ceiling pointing at the earth after the bombing but I probably heard stories of that sort. It refers to religious pictures with angels flapping around and pointing their finger in the sky or down to the earth, like a token of assurance of the world being in God's hands. But there it is a dead corpse on the rafters pointing down as a *memento mori*, as a reminder of the total situation. To be a survivor was very significant for me, but I suppose that growing up expecting to see ruined houses all around gave me a sense of the apocalyptic. If I was born in the 1880s I would have had it from the Bible – the Day of Wrath and all that. When you live in an age of newsreels and photographs you are conscious with your feet, you must be standing somewhere.

In what way is it so specific?

Because at the end of the war, there were these newspaper photographs of Nazi atrocities. These pictures have now become commonplace and I don't think you can know the impression they made, how startling and unexpected they once were. Until then, images had been tame, few and subdued – today's blot out their own reality and have even changed the human voice, made it more mechanical so that we often sound like machines laughing or crying. Then one day in the newspapers in which, in those war days, you ate your fish-and-chips, there were these photographs. It was as if the war you had lived through had been only a sheet that had been ripped away in a final unveiling (as for a monument) and underneath was this ultimate horror. At that moment the world became old and mankind unfathomable. It was the ground zero of the human soul, the ice at the bottom of Dante's hell. I remember in particular a series of pictures of people (concentration camp inmates) who had been crowded into a barn by SS men who then set fire to it. I remember one man sitting on a box, who had been charred so that his flesh and clothes all seemed to be made of the same stuff – like a bronze statue. He was leaning forward and resting his chin on his hand exactly like Rodin's *Thinker*. I hadn't then seen this statue but I could see what Rodin had seen *before* it existed. In the inferno it seemed that this man had sat down and contemplated all the things that are of concern. This would have been accidental – obviously he died in torment. Yet for me it was the real fulcrum of reality, a point in the chaos where you can set the lever. And so this image has always been important for me.

Some forty years later you used this figure in one of your War Plays, Red, Black and Ignorant. *You called him 'The Monster' and he is a child that had been charred to death in a future nuclear Armageddon and he comes on stage to tell and understand what happens in the audience's life to allow this.*

For this character I had also been very influenced by the drawings of the survivors of Hiroshima. When I looked at them, I had the feeling these people were asking questions about their own life. But the meaning of these things can change very quickly. When I wrote the play with the Monster in the early 80s, our main problem was the threat of nuclear war. It was pervasive like a ghost, getting everywhere. You had this feeling of living on the edge of catastrophe as if some medieval plague was striking city after city – Cambridge, at the end of this road, with its universities and colleges, was a target for Soviet nuclear missiles and some distance in the other direction there were two air force bases, with bombers ready to annihilate Russia. The play was dealing directly with that situation but it also tried to contain it by being more objective and with lyricism, as if it was saying: 'Don't panic'. But when it was staged last year in London, the absence of the Cold War was very noticeable and I wanted to open it to present disasters. So instead of the Monster producing the ashes of the world blown up by global nuclear blast as in the original, now at the end the whole cast scattered ashes while evoking symbols of waste and nothingness. However, all these things we could at that time see in the newsreel created an unfathomable sense of disaster. Really, we all died in Auschwitz. I sometimes think humanity itself died there. It didn't make any sense. Instead of the devil lurking somewhere around ready to catch you, suddenly we were confronted with the totality of evil. It was there as a fact even though you had survived.

Did these war experiences in your youth contribute to you wanting to become a writer?

Such experiences create a gap in which you can watch other people and their reactions, what they are doing. Being bombed very young gave me this ability to understand what my characters do in a situation by putting myself into it. It doesn't mean if you want to be a dramatist you have to get yourself bombed! There are millions of other ways of putting yourself in the truth of the situation. But it can't be evaded. However, I never *wanted* to become a writer. I found I was one. In my twenties I wrote poetry. My idol was Rimbaud. I wanted to write poetry that would just consist of looking round me and really to see and in a way celebrate what was there. It seems a paradoxical thing to say but it's true: there also was a sense of enjoyment in that war situation; the danger didn't get you, it is possible to exist. It is totally different from the atmosphere of false gaiety we constantly live in nowadays which ignores reality. Our society lives totally without happiness. So creating poetry could have really been an alternative to the genuine happiness of surviving in war and a stand against its absolute horror. So I sort of emulated Rimbaud until I went into the army.

You were called up for military service in the early 50s for two years. You spent them in the Allied occupation forces in Vienna.

Yes. I then became a trained killer: I wore a uniform, I had a gun, I learned how to throw a hand grenade, how to bayonet somebody. I used a lot of that in the bayonet lesson in my play *Eleven Vests*: the screaming, the violence you have to use to cut out the enemy's guts – though the Instructor would put the language into obscenities which I couldn't use as I was writing for a young audience. I also knew the camaraderie of killing: how people would support the demand to kill made on them by inventing some unity within the group. I didn't kill anyone but I was aware of it. I was faced with a new problem: 'You are now a killer. What do you think of that?' Then poetry ceased for me to be possible. There was no system that could hold the world together. It was no longer sufficient to observe: I had to participate in the act of observation. Instead of a poetry celebrating the world of appearance, achieving a *joie de vivre* through observation, I needed a poetry of involvement that could penetrate the situation, enter the invisible world, the no man's land, the gap, where meaning stands or can be created. This gap appears everywhere and this is what Hitler was claiming to own or Stalin – or Mrs Thatcher, to go from the grandiose to the ridiculous. Poetry has to be spoken inside this gap. So it became necessary for me to create drama. Poetry of Rimbaud's sort, as commentary, as observation has been finally made impossible by the modern consumer world. Everything becomes a product, a commodity, an exchange value, and becomes ugly. All this rush of activity and technological know-how and power being released, all these artefacts, this world of things, are like those scaffoldings we see surrounding buildings in construction, but they are scaffolds around nothing: it doesn't build a world of values. Poetry is only possible now if it belongs to drama.

You often refer to a performance of Macbeth *by Donald Wolfit you saw with your school in your teens as your first and very striking dramatic experience. Did it have this involvement effect on you that you describe?*

This was a very important experience for me. It was the first time I heard someone talking about the life I had lived, about the politics, the society around me. It was a sense of total recognition. That was actually my world, I knew these people: they were in the streets or in the newspaper. I knew the witches flying in the night because I had known about German airmen trying to kill me. I had been wondering why these people up there were doing that and here was a man in this play killing children. My reactions were very naive but after the performance I had a feeling of resolution. I could understand the world I was in, how the bits and pieces of the world integrated themselves. I knew there were certain standards and if one could maintain these, they could work in a social situation. So I could say: 'Well, yes, I know what I have to do, what it means to be alive.' Afterwards it was a real surprise that other people who saw it could go on with their lives as before.

Was it because of the play or was there something specific in the performance?

Wolfit's performance had a sense of human dignity. Macbeth is like

Adolf Hitler: he is a murderer but he is the wisest and the most human character in the play. He is the person who has far and away the most insight and he has all the soliloquies, just like Hamlet. That is really what Shakespeare is about. Shakespeare is not interested in the divine but in morality because it is what human beings create. I now understand Macbeth better – he is both Hamlet and Claudius.

In what sense do you mean this?

Macbeth seems to be about the supernatural but it is about the nature of human beings. Any other dramatist would have made the witches come back, at the coronation feast for example. So why does Shakespeare get bored with them? Witches are the supernatural power and they have to do with the meaning of life or fate, like St Augustin's predestination. The witches are God's property. But Shakespeare knows that the problem stands 'not in our stars but in ourselves' – to quote *Julius Caesar*. He is interested in the individual; he wants to know what a human being is – the same questions Oedipus asks. So Macbeth has to look into himself, not at the witches. Then he finds two problems: authenticity and power – the personal and the political. The play moves from the political to the personal in order to understand the political. You don't need witches to explore that.

But still Macbeth is chased by ghosts and strange apparitions – so are Hamlet and Richard III.

Of course, but a ghost is personal. It is the return of your own actions or your own repressed. See Lady Macbeth: she is haunted, not by the witches but by her own actions. The ghosts are really Macbeth's or Hamlet's conscience – all ghosts are really yourself. Of course we are scared of ghosts but we are happy to have them because they give sense to our life. What do you do when you see a ghost? You run away. Shakespeare's characters do the opposite: Hamlet doesn't run away, he goes into the problem. Lady Macbeth is the toughest and the most brutal in that couple, but her sleep reveals she *knows* what she did and faces it. Macbeth never denies what he is doing or gives deceiving reasons –'I am doing this out of love' or 'because God told me to'. He says: 'This is what I am doing.' And he pursues that trajectory as far as he can for the audience's sake. He takes them on that journey into that situation, to its extreme, and there he finds the language to explain what is happening to him. He eventually realizes he has trapped himself and he then finds a curious form of innocence. That's what drama does: it penetrates the situation rather than adjusting it. Our problem is that we live in violent situations – and we have to write about this. Saints have nothing interesting to say to us. But Macbeths do.

That is the attitude of your plays towards the violence of our times: they mean to really face it as it actually is and as human actions.

It is said that the Emperor Claudius, who didn't like the arena, made himself go because he considered you had to face the worst your age can produce. So it is absolutely necessary as part of your moral responsibility to face up to the extreme experiences of your age. The tragic sense is also the moral sense; both go together. I lived in a century of cemeteries and I can't be silent about that. If you have the ability to write plays that is what you should use it for. My concern is for all the people who are not yet born: will they live in times as horrendous as those in the past? I am conscious of this when I'm writing: we have moral responsibility.

That moral responsibility of the writer is what you put at stake in your play Bingo. *And you had the nerve to choose to question it through the most iconic writer of English literature: William Shakespeare.*

It is said that there are three important books in English literature: King James' Bible, the works of Darwin and Shakespeare's plays. Shakespeare is so completely dominant: he has a play on every subject, on every occasion. Every time you open a door, you find he is already there. He says: 'Do you know what life is? Life is this! Do you know what death is? Death is this! Do you know what a battle is? A battle is this! Do you know what love is? Love is this!' He would have a serious answer for any significant thing you would deal with and you have to knock him off his pedestal in some way. You can make jokes or parodies about him, he remains God. And if you have the temerity to say he doesn't understand something, people don't take you seriously. In *Bingo*, I made Ben Jonson say the moment someone mentions Shakespeare, something happens to the group and everybody's eyes change. Jonson thinks Shakespeare comes from another world, he could walk on water – and he carries a mat with him so that he can wipe his feet and not dirty the water! That is how the good London literati looked at Shakespeare. Among all the people he met in London, Jonson was the one who knew most who he was talking to. Shakespeare is a bit like Racine and Molière in one person. But Racine is more like God's dentist: he knows where the teeth are and checks if they are all in their right place. Whereas Shakespeare is God's chiropodist: he is interested in His feet. He has corns and blisters but He has to walk, to go on a journey.

Shakespeare is such a good dramatist because he always has the ability to see reality and to speak through the eyes of his characters. He is always authentic. Half of what he says is totally incoherent to an English audience today, partly because it is almost in a foreign language. This enables performers to over-relish their performance so that it is sometimes just like spoken opera. But the other half of his language you could hear it in the tube station and in the supermarket now. It is a strange combination of a totally demotic language and this huge elevated effulgence of a very metaphorical language which is not open to writers and audiences any more – because the metaphors have been destroyed by science.

One cannot say you are particularly indulgent or deferential towards him in this play. You show him as a wealthy landlord, indifferent to, if not complicit with, the violence that happens around and even quite close to him.

Shakespeare always deals with problems he finds difficult. In his plays you find people in disguise, mad people, very strange violence and fools running around. In my play, I wanted to see how his problems appear in his life, what difficulties it makes for him when these are presented to him in real life. He lived in a time of huge civil unrest (twenty years after his death the country was at civil war) and he was surrounded by all these Tudor gangsters. Really – Stalin's agents were amateurs compared to these thugs, but he asked if it was possible for somebody really to act on moral grounds; it is obvious in *Measure for Measure*, for example. Then it is also notorious that the only specimens of Shakespeare's handwriting are signatures on legal documents, among them one which deals with land he happened to own on the local heath. It was the time when the enclosures started and the other landlords wanted him to agree that he wouldn't interfere with the legal steps they would take to drive people off their lands. He signed this document and kept his mouth shut. This is what I show in *Bingo*. I did some research: everything I say about it in the play is absolutely true. In my play Shakespeare is not especially happy about it but he does it in order to have financial security. Nobody is interested in Shakespeare as a writer, except Jonson. At the end of the scene when they meet in an inn, he asks for one thing, one *word*, from him – and all Shakespeare does is put money on the table. Shakespeare's problem is that he felt he could collect the money and still be a poet – but money in our society is a form of violence.

In the play, almost immediately after Shakespeare signed his paper, a Young Woman turns up in Shakespeare's garden. She is begging and prostituting herself and she will be persecuted to death.

She is an illegal immigrant really (because it was a capital offence then to travel from one town to another without a passport) and she is eventually hanged. In the immediate situation, she is a victim of the enclosures so Shakespeare can then see the consequence of what he became complicit in and realize his moral involvement in her death. Later on, he also sees another result of his actions when the peasants join up on the side of the Puritans, who are true religious fanatics. Shakespeare hates them (they wanted to close all the theatres anyway) but this shows the cultural effects of his practical decisions. These fanatics are creatures and propagators of the culture that allows the landlords and the peasants who are natural enemies to exist together in one society. He then realizes that the peasants are turning their backs on him because they see him as their enemy now. When he meets them in the inn they hide from him and whisper – though they used to take their hats off to him. He says: 'Now people have to lie to me.' That is one of the things he loses by signing this document. It deeply saddens him. But in the play, I wanted to allow Shakespeare to criticize himself.

How will he manage to do this?

In the first part of the play, he sits silently on his bench in his garden, just like a spectator of a play that he had written himself – but he hears every syllable even when he doesn't seem to and is very conscious of everything happening around him. Shakespeare is an observer – if you write a play like *King Lear*, you must know about what is going on in other people's lives. But that isn't Lear: Lear goes out on the heath and rages against the injustice of society and the cruelty of God. It is a split between Lear and Shakespeare, a contradiction between what Shakespeare said as a dramatist and what he did as a property owner.

You show how silent and passive he can be in a scene where he is directly confronted both with the dead body of the Young Woman exposed on her gibbet up on a hill and the Puritans taking a grip on the peasants who went to see her execution. And he doesn't have a word against it.

No. It is true he could have said something about the Young Woman hanging and the land being stolen – crimes occurring on that hill and in his garden. But instead he has this huge harangue about the crimes in London and the audience watching a bear being tortured. This, by the way, is true (you can still see the pit beside the Globe today in London): the place for bear baiting actually stood so close to his theatre that Shakespeare would have been literally able to hear them – the performances of his plays would have been like a chamber music orchestra playing in the room next to a football crowd. So, he attacks his society's barbarities, and blames people for not saying 'no' to those – whereas he himself had said 'yes' by signing the document – *but* then he talks about the bear. He is becoming like a character in one of his own plays. He knows what King Lear says and why he says it, so he is trapped by his own plays because he realizes his plays are better than he is. It is as if he was in a law court and he had sworn an oath on his plays. He begins to see that he is implicated in all that and has to accept his part in the responsibility for it. Now he asks himself: 'Are my plays true? Are they making true statements about reality or are they false?'

That is why he keeps repeating 'Was anything done?' throughout the last scenes of the play?

This line comes from Leonardo da Vinci's Notebooks. Leonardo invented the aeroplane, the helicopter, the tank and then he said: 'Have I done anything? Was it worthwhile?' Only an exceptional man has the modesty to ask himself that. It is a question that Shakespeare could very much ask himself: 'You wrote *Hamlet*, *Macbeth* ... does it mean anything? Was it worth it?' And his answer would be: 'Yes, but you also signed that paper.' If you put that on the balance as a crime and everything else on the other side, the crime will keep swinging the balance. *That* sentences him to death. So everything has to go into that decision and it conspires to force Shakespeare to look at himself and his life. He comes to a sort of Nietzschean conclusion that there is no god, no moral end of the universe. He says earlier on: 'To have usurped the place of God and lied ...'; in other words: 'I have acted like God by writing plays that would tell the meaning of life, but it was all a lie.' He steps out of the boundary of theatre into the street and real life. So he wants to prove to himself that it is possible to make a moral gesture. He considers what he did was inhuman – for him this is like claiming the world is square: he has to take himself seriously. And so to be serious he kills himself.

Why should he need to kill himself to be serious?

His suicide proves that *he is* wrong when he signs the paper and *his plays* are right. By signing the paper, he is inconsistent with *King Lear* – but by killing himself he is consistent with *King Lear*. It is a deliberate act to give meaning to his life and so to human life. This is *always* misunderstood: people believe he commits suicide out of despair. He doesn't. The one thing Shakespeare never does is despair. People believe what they *think* they are told, not what they are *really* being told. They usually can tell the meaning of a situation, but I am presenting them with situations so that they can change their meaning. So it depends on how it is acted. Everything always does.

THE ONE THING SHAKESPEARE NEVER DOES IS DESPAIR

Shakespeare kills himself in the middle of an argument between the leader of the Puritans and the leader of the landlords.

He kills himself because of that. There is not a right side of the argument because both of these people would kill somebody else to maintain their systems of faith and both are responsible for hanging the Young Woman. Shakespeare is caught between the two – they are literally arguing above his head and he stays in the middle. He cannot unravel this political situation of the year 1616, but he can say that what is at stake in it is the unlocking of that confusion between those two people.

This is preceded by a pictorially very strong and very suggestively meditating scene. Shakespeare is drunk (he comes from the inn he was in with Ben Jonson) and tries to find his way home on the pure white snow that covers everything.

In the previous scene, Shakespeare saw the social relationships in the town breaking down and he has been told by Jonson (who hates him and loves him because he wrote those plays) that he is such a great writer. Now he is left apart and he is drunk but at least it gives him time to be with himself and to listen to himself and to look at himself as a writer. So the reality of his life begins to unfold. He has a Hamlet soliloquy with himself and tells himself who he is and what he has done; he talks about the meaning of his life and the meaning of his own actions. He remembers the first poem he ever wrote and says if he were a young man he would write a sonnet about what has happened because then he could respond to it in his freedom. But now he has the burden of the ultimate seriousness of the world. So the scene is like a review of his life and demonstrates that Shakespeare knew that when he signed that paper he killed his own childhood, his youth. But every sane man – certainly every good writer – must be true to the vision of their youth. So Shakespeare can face the determinant moral problems of his situation and he comes to understand his culpability with great clarity. Then he meets his old gardener, whose mind was damaged during the war – the old man is like a child and Shakespeare plays snowballs with him.

He will be killed soon after by a stray bullet from a confrontation between the peasants and the landlords' guards. It is actually happening close by. All the audience see of this are vague human figures running behind Shakespeare's back, who, once more, doesn't seem to notice

Shakespeare talks about the birds that will freeze to death tonight (referring to the biblical line that says God is aware of the fall of every sparrow), but in reality nobody would know or care for them – and the Old Man is about to die in that snow. It is the opposite, nightmarish, image he mentioned earlier in the play of the swan flying along the river – which in part referred to himself.

What is the point in putting this meditation in this set all covered with pure white snow? It seems very unreal – and as a deadly fight takes place that will kill the Old Man.

Well, first of all, it did actually snow in April when Shakespeare died; it is historically true. Then it makes a light scene after the scene in the inn just before that was dark, suddenly this shocking light, nothing is hidden. The snow is like a great sheet of paper – because Shakespeare is a man who lives on paper. He could use the snow to write about the reality of his life. If he commits a crime in his life, that is on the paper. And if he is really writing the truth on it, then the reality and his own involvement in it would write themselves on it as well. It becomes a place where morality has presence. You can't escape that. So he can't have a clean sheet as if he were sitting in his study with the freedom to write. The privilege of the writer turns into the responsibility of the writer. He might think: 'I meant this and in fifty years' time it would have another significance.' But what it really means is: '*I* signed that paper, *she* was hanged.' The sheet of snow represents the poet and on it the violence of his life and times is presented to him in glimpses of men running away, being chased by other men with guns. Instead of sitting at his desk and writing on it, *he* is the ink on the paper: *his life*, with all its determinant events, is now writing itself on the paper. His life is writing *him* on the sheet of paper and the play is writing the audience's life on the stage. The play intervenes on their imagination like the figures running across the stage in the play. It's not the romantic idea of the poet writing with his own blood. He writes with other people's blood.

2
WHAT IS TERRIBLE ABOUT EVIL IS NOT THAT IT IS BANAL BUT THAT IT IS DOMESTICATED

The Fool: the poet and the revolution, to act and to know / 'You had a poet in your field my lord!' / Dominating by deference / The Parson's martyr / *Restoration*: the killing of two working-class people, the cynical and the submitted / Whose benefit are the hangings? / Lord Are and the spirit of Restoration comedies / *The Sea*: Mrs Rafi, the local Queen Victoria / Optimism and pessimism, the play-inside-the-play-inside-the-play / 'Ha, ha' / Hatch, the outcast in the class struggle / A velvet tempest / The drowned man, another childhood memory.

After Bingo, *you wrote another play,* The Fool, *which also questions the role of the writer in society through a second classical figure of English literature, but diametrically opposed to Shakespeare, the peasant poet John Clare.*

Shakespeare was an affluent writer and Clare was a working-class writer. He was like one of the peasants that Shakespeare wanted to drive off the land and in this play the enclosures movement is still the driving force. He lived in the Fens which is an area I was at home in because it is where my parents come from. Shakespeare destroys himself but only in order to save himself. With Clare it is the other way round. He too lived in an increasingly anti-human set-up and he tried to live a human life by breaking the customary rules of his community. But he couldn't break them totally and was destroyed by his society. He ended locked away in a madhouse. I wanted to show the effect all that has on his private life and also how he became a danger to his own family. There are things you can't compromise with. The play is written to find some function for poetry in that situation.

In your play Clare is involved in a revolutionary action. The first part of the play deals directly with the historic Littleport riots of 1816 and focuses very much on a leader of the rioters you called Darkie, who is Clare's closest friend and who is hanged.

The riots occurred because the working peasants' land was being stolen and they were forced off it and driven into towns. I decided to put it together with the story of John Clare because in his poetry he is protesting about what is happening to the peasants' lives. But factually they are two separate events. The name 'Clare' sounds like 'light' – it suggests clarity – and I invented 'Darkie' as an opposite to him. Clare is the poet, that is understanding, interpretation ('light'). This is my question: How to stop recreating the problem, especially as it relates to what I called in an essay 'The Faustian Trap'. Clare had to be shut up just as Darkie had to be hanged – at that time they didn't hang poets because ideology was more certain of its power. At the end in his asylum he can't talk and only produces the throat sounds that hanged people make.

What makes them opposite then?

Clare's and Darkie's are two conflicting positions. In a late scene of the play, that happens in his head, Clare meets Darkie again and he says to him: 'You are the one who acts, but you don't see where you are going. You don't see the consequences of your action.' If the conversation had gone on Darkie would have said: 'Yes, but I know where I stand, I know where I am.' Instead he knocks Clare out, because he is useless in that situation. Clare then answers – and this is probably the central line of the play: 'I am a poet and I teach men how to eat bread.' Both their lives are wasted because they are two necessary parts of action and they aren't joined. The play says each needs the other and they shouldn't be divided. But at that time they could only be put together in madhouses or prisons. We shouldn't have illusions. Clare and Darkie pose our problem for us but they are not its solution.

What makes Clare's position as a poet socially critical in the play?

Clare wanted to bring realism into pastoral poetry; he always spoke of real matters. This made it subversive – we don't realize how much this was so. Up until the middle of the nineteenth century, the English Romantic movement involved itself in this poetry of nature, influenced by Classical Roman writers like Catullus or Virgil's *Eclogues* – partly because with the Industrial Revolution, the middle classes began to think about what they might be losing with the countryside. But it was a form of idealism, of escapism. Clare's poetry was the opposite of this. He talked about economic reality and wrote you have mud on your boots if you cross a field. If Shakespeare thought art holds a mirror up to nature, Clare would think art is *involved* in it. In the play one of his sponsors in the upper class, Mrs Emmerson (who is a historical character) is in raptures to see the spirit of nature coming through this man who couldn't even wash his hands properly. This is wonderful! Unfortunately he has political ideas …

We meet her in a scene staged in Hyde Park as she and another of his rich literary sponsors try to talk Clare into making his writing politically acceptable. At the same time, upstage, there is a boxing match between two starving men, pushed to fight by their own backers to get a meal.

The audience can see the similarity between the two and realizes that Clare is in the same position as the boxers. They are being exploited in the same way by their backers. The one who loses the fight won't get a meal and later on Clare will starve because his backers refuse to pay for his poetry if it doesn't fit in with their wishes. In this scene, Clare has not yet realized this, he is not yet defeated, but his backers are already destroying him. They are not interested in what his art really is. The boxer who will lose fights very bitterly; he manages to crawl to his feet, like someone crawling out of his coffin. His power of resistance impresses Clare very much. Later on, when he appears to be the most beaten and the most down, Clare would demonstrate the same power of resistance. He takes over the whole play and he has a speech of huge arrogance to his landlord, as if he was in a pulpit addressing the congregation: 'You had a poet in your field my lord!' He means: 'I stand here, with the authority of a poet and it is greater than your authority.' It is because he defied him and his society in that way that he is sent into the madhouse. If he had been working in a factory he might have become some sort of revolutionary. He wanted to be a poet and the political identity of the poet hadn't been worked out – if it ever has been. He was stranded between two worlds. In the end he is the author of his own madness. He could have done the prudent thing and apologize for his behaviour, but he says: 'No: the authority of creativity has to be heard.'

So Clare is subversive not only as a creative person, but as a creative working-class *person. He establishes and gives evidence of the creativity of the working class which is not meant to be creative.*

In *The Fool* I wanted to show the self-repression of the working class. You don't step out of line, you don't come into conflict with a squire, you keep your nose clean. Of course peasants shouldn't read – at the most they should read the Bible. Life was very controlled in that way, mainly by deference. Deference was a mass phenomenon and a very important element in society. You would defer to authority figures for two reasons. One is that they control your life anyway so if you aren't deferential to the boss you'd get sacked. Be deferential if you want to eat. The second is: in some matters they actually do know better. They go to university, they have the educated intelligence, the insight and the understanding. A friend of mine from the working class became very angry because when he told the milkman he was going to university, the milkman replied he himself was too stupid to be anything except the milkman. This man could grin and say he was stupid – but if you told him he had bad breath he would probably have punched you on the nose.

WHAT IS TERRIBLE ABOUT IT IS BANAL

The play opens with another very specific demonstration of the creativity of the working class. We attend a peasants' Christmas performance of a 'Mummers' Play' at the gate of Lord Milton's castle. This is a little popular drama: they have beautiful costumes and they act and sing with beautiful music the victory of St George over the dragon.

All these various abilities in the rural communities have been destroyed and now people, instead of being creators in that way, are turned into spectators of modern sports or musicals. Those 'Mummers' Plays' are genuine and they had their origins in medieval drama. The peasants would adapt them to recent events, in this play the Napoleonic wars: brave John Bull beating all these French froggies. It is reduced to an ideological celebration of England's victory that demonstrates unity between the squires, the aristocrats and the working class. But because the pressures on the peasants of industrialization and poverty are increasing, the scene, instead of paying homage to Lord Milton, turns into a quarrel in which Darkie attacks his ideology – its castle in the sky, and its fantasy version of England. Milton and the aristocrats can still retreat into his mansion. What Darkie says doesn't matter to him. But he leaves the Parson alone with them. The Parson works as an intermediary between Milton and the peasants, interpreting Milton's argument in a patronizing way which he hopes the peasants will accept. But he doesn't have a mansion or a castle, he only has a church.

During the riot scene the Parson is the one to be exposed instead of his masters. The peasants catch him as he tries to run away and rather than beating or killing him, they decide to strip him, piece by piece, so that he ends naked among them.

The scene is like an unveiling ceremony for a sculpture. It dramatizes the breaking down of social order and for the peasants it is a much more complex problem to deal with than having a riot. It is a very difficult for them to cross the space from where they are standing to where the Parson is. They feel almost like bomb disposal experts: if they touch the Parson, the bomb explodes. It involves a lot of silence – if the actors jump across the stage to tear his clothes off in excitement, it doesn't work – and as they proceed and take his clothes off, they are astonished by the expensive underclothes, then the flesh that is so carefully looked after, pampered, and so on ... And they see more and more of themselves in contrast. They realize he has stolen not only the wealth they could have earned with their work but even their own flesh. All of them are totally concentrated on him so that they forget one of them has been seriously wounded in the riot and is crawling very slowly across the stage dragging the sheet that had been wrapped around his head – and by the end of the scene he will be dead – without anybody noticing him – except the audience. He is a constant reminder, like a wound moving across the stage, whereas the Parson is losing only his sense of self-respect or authority.

What effect does this action have on the Parson?

The Parson wears his ideology's uniform, so when the peasants stripped him they trampled on his ideology and undermined it. Then he would hold on to the strongest part of his ideology, which is death: later on, when Darkie learns he will hang, the Parson thinks he is the lucky one because he will suffer on the scaffold and be closer to God – and he is in rapture when he receives that special mission to go to the scaffold with him! But his most enigmatic speech is when Clare has been taken to the madhouse. As long as Milton is there he behaves like a Parson and says all the right theological things. But once Milton has gone he says: 'Tragedy is like justice: blind and over pity. Clare didn't ask for help ... he scorned us ... In a way his sufferings condemn him. They protect him with the arrogance of a certain sort of pain.' It is a very sinister nihilistic insight but there is a sort of strange and subtle truth in it too, to say his sufferings are what protect him from suffering. How can his sufferings turn into arrogance? This is something dangerously malignant to say that at that moment, because everybody would just pity Clare – and that is what the audience should do. I think the devil is a more profound psychologist than God – in fact I think the devil invented God to torment mankind.

This deference and its false unity are clearly exposed in your play Restoration. *It is set in the eighteenth century and we follow Bob Hedges and Frank, the two servants of the infamous Lord Are, each having the opposite attitude towards him. At the end he has the two hanged together.*

WHAT IS TERRIBLE ABOUT IT IS BANAL

Bob is the loyal working-class guy, Frank is the cynical one – he thinks you have to get what you can for yourself. In one scene, he steals some of the lord's cutlery and Bob Hedges and his mother make a big effort to catch him and lock him in a chest. Then they go off to get the police and Frank is left alone in the box in the middle of the stage. The stage directions say: he bangs on the sides, on the bottom, he knocks on the top, he talks, shouts, knocks, stamps, then silence, you might think he's dead, then he claps his hands, and so on. It is very elaborate because I want the audience to watch somebody banging hard inside a box for five minutes and see that this man has spent his life in a situation of repression, in prison – all the working-class characters have. He is usually very clever and adroit in manipulating things, he is 'Jack-the-Lad', a comic all over the place. But in the box, he is like someone in the stocks and is almost crippled by his social situation. He has energy and wit, but no opportunity to use this creatively. So I put him in a box. Bob is outside the box but he is as much in the box as Frank. He acts as a jailer but he is a prisoner of the situation and so is his mother. She can't even count but she knows when a spoon is missing – you *can* teach a dog tricks ...

During the play, Lord Are murders his wife – in quite ridiculous circumstances – and Bob Hedges is so deferential towards him that he agrees to be charged in his place for this crime.

The important point is Bob Hedges's psychological situation. Lord Are told him he will protect him if he admits guilt, so that the image of law and order won't be tarnished. The question is: will he? won't he? say what really happened? His wife, Rose, wants him to whereas his mother doesn't because she thinks it wouldn't get him anywhere. The expectation of the audience would be that Bob Hedges will get away and this breaks down only when he refuses to escape with Rose, though he has everything ready for it: the door is open, so is the window, but he gave his promise to this man who is authority and he has to trust him. He is trapped because obviously Lord Are will let him be hanged to get rid of him. He is very friendly with him and pats him on his shoulder, but Bob Hedges is shackled – you see him literally with chains on his feet. When I directed the play at the Royal Court, I had Bob walk along the stage when Are says: 'You are an Englishman and all the Englishmen are free', so that you could hear the chains rattling. Hedges isn't able to change his view of the world: he is not claiming his innocence but his corruption. You also see how Bob's mother is being abused and exploited. She contributes to the murder when she burns Bob's pardon because Lord Are told her to and since she can't read she couldn't know what it was. I had in mind working-class people who voted for Hitler – or, if it comes to that, for Thatcher.

Bob Hedges won't revolt ever, not even at the very moment he is led to the scaffold.

When the play drove him to his extreme, he turns into the hero who decides to put on a good show – and he claims 'Hang me high!' You could say: 'This guy is capable of great courage' or: 'Bloody fool! Is that the best you can do?' It is appalling. His behaviour is the opposite of Darkie's in *The Fool*: his sister Patty brought him his best jacket so that he can be hanged decently dressed and doesn't 'disgrace the family' – like a child who has to come on a stage to receive his certificate for passing his exams. He refuses the jacket and gives it to Clare instead. Darkie knows his situation and where his enemies are. Bob never has and he thinks Lord Are will protect him. He ends up celebrating his own hanging. Darkie will never put on a performance for them in what he calls 'their circus'.

In The Fool *(to stay with it for a moment since we are back to it) there is a situation quite similar where the Littleport rioters are waiting for their execution. But the scene develops differently. A pardon unexpectedly arrives for everybody but Darkie. As the news spreads a huge burst of laughter contaminates the whole prison and its echoes run around the only man who actually will hang.*

All the prisoners who were about to die five minutes before, are now told they are free! They keep saying to Darkie they are so sorry and they desperately can't stop laughing. Even Clare, the most sympathetic character, who needs to understand most in the play, is falling over with laughter. But the jailer is really worried. Not that somebody will lose their life, but that he may lose his job because of the disorder this laughter makes. Normally he just stands by the door but the laughter makes

WHAT IS TERRIBLE ABOUT IT IS BANAL

him cross the cell to threaten Clare face to face: 'You stop laughing because you're damaging my job' – not: 'You shouldn't laugh in the presence of somebody who's going to be hanged.' This shows where the jailer stands.

Another character tries to have them stop: Darkie's sister Patty, who is devastated.

She came to console her brother but she eventually quarrelled with him and all she does is clear up the soup dishes. She doesn't know how to deal with having shouted at someone who is about to be hanged so she becomes the housewife and she starts clearing up the place. This tells you what these people's lives are about. The cruelty that happens in homes depends on those things in their lives. And Clare notices a fly going in and out the bars – nobody else does. He can't not mention the fly, because he is a poet and that is what he notices. He would say the fly desires freedom like human beings desire laughter. So, because the keeper is worried about his job, because Patty has no language (she's not a poet) to say she is sorry she shouted, because Clare can notice the fly but has no one to say it to, because of all those things Darkie will be hanged. The scene takes these bits apart from each character's social situation and shows how they are assembled.

In Restoration *we don't see the warden, but there is another character who is not involved in the execution on a moral ground at all, but just does her job. This is the hangman's wife who is busy selling beer to those who attend the execution.*

Of course, because she runs the inn where the hangman lives. So they both make money from the hanging: he with his salary and she by selling beer. She is morally implicated in the hanging because she profits from it and she would like more hangings, so that she could buy new curtains – *hanging* curtains … The scene is built on how much beer she can sell: each time she sells one she chalks it up on a board. So that we see the hanging is good for her, good for business, good for the Parson. The hangman is never seen in the play but his wife is because she is the economic reality of this business of hanging people. It is not the macabre side of things, but the domestic side of things, the domestication of evil. What is terrible about evil is not that it is banal but that it is domesticated. Ironically, Hedges also drinks – and Frank is drunk. So even the condemned are increasing the profit she made out of the hanging. It is the position of the working class.

Bob has his wife here, Rose, who doesn't behave like Darkie's sister but who supports him fiercely. She is a very unexpected working-class character, not only because she is politically conscious and opposes her masters to try to save Bob, but also because she is black.

I needed somebody who would be outside that particular class relationship so that she could see it differently and be aware of what is going on. But she had to be acceptable within that world. An English politically conscious woman just wouldn't be there – just as Lord Milton wouldn't have Darkie as his butler. This is why she is a black character. This also makes her invisible – so she is licensed. When she says things like, 'You can't treat Bob Hedges that way', the others would just think she doesn't know what she is talking about because she is black. From the point of view of the aristocracy she would be like Lear's Fool: no one would take her seriously. As a black woman she also knows what slavery is so she can see the reality of Bob Hedges's situation. She tells him: 'You are a slave but don't know it.' She is also the one who decides to set Frank free from his chest, although she is worried about the conflict this will cause with her husband and about endangering her own situation in the house.

It is strange, by the way, that this play which is supposed to be a revival of a Restoration comedy, which is a very codified and self-celebrating aristocratic genre, is so focused on genuine working-class characters.

That is why I wrote it. It was commissioned to be part of a season of traditional English Restoration comedies, as a 'modern' one, and I took it as an opportunity to approach it in a different way. I didn't need to satirize the genre because it satirizes itself: it is a theatre of self-congratulatory, self-admiring society with a confidence that reverses the revolution – the monarchy is restored, the aristocrats have got rid of the Puritans and Oliver Cromwell, they can go to the theatre again and they can make themselves rich. It is like being in the French Second Empire:

things are back to what they always should be. I put this genre in the social and political reality of the servants so that it is no longer self-indulging. You wouldn't see anything like the hanging of Bob Hedges in a Restoration comedy – they concentrate only on the rich aristocracy. Nevertheless I do like them! They are very funny and often very well written. Some of them, like Wycherley or Congreve's *The Way of The World*, are almost like Oscar Wilde: it is high comedy; the language is very elegant, very 'knowing'. It is also very satirical and sardonic. It is an amazing self-portrait caricature of the aristocracy, with heirs waiting to get the money and these grotesque fops and idiotic women. It is not really critical of the society it portrays, it just shows it to be ridiculous. In this sense its satire is really cynical, but not consciously. I like its insouciance, its ability to just carry on without noticing the carnage it is spreading around. It is a relief after the Puritans.

Your play shows quite clearly this superbly careless confidence through this character of Lord Are. He is a very colourful and monstrous mixture of wit, ridicule, self-indulgence, inventiveness and in the end vicious violence.

I liked very much writing Lord Are: he is typical of Restoration comedies, with his ability to survive, whatever happens – his wife is murdered: he just has to ring the bell and get the servant to come and confess to it. What shocks him is not that his wife is murdered (by him, incidentally) but that she is murdered before breakfast. It is not the done thing: you should at least wait until the afternoon … This upsets all the rest of the day. To allow yourself to be murdered before breakfast shows a lack of breeding.

He is also highly imaginative. In a memorable speech, we see him inventing all sorts of implausible stories in order to persuade a messenger to give him the pardon for Bob – and then destroy it. And once he has got it in his hands he still goes on, figuring out a glorious future. His imagination seems to have become so prodigiously active he can't stop it.

He should think immediately of how to get rid of the pardon, but he gets excited by his ideas and his mind still rushes on, exploring all the possibilities of the future. It is his sheer power of invention. All he describes could actually happen in a Restoration play but he goes one step further and celebrates this power. He says: 'O thou great blazing sun! Great fire of everlasting day! My life! My ministering star! Blaze! Blaze! Blaze! Blaze! Hail great sun! Light of the world that I shall stride in!' Are becomes a heroic figure between a Shakespeare character and William Blake's Satan, the irresistible force of the Industrial Revolution and the British Empire: he is going to take over the globe. And then he says to the audience: 'O my friends –', but he is lost for words. And at this climax of self-celebration, he becomes petty – about a button missing from his coat; he rages hysterically against Bob's mother who should have sewn it on. He possesses the world and believes he can do anything, but a button is missing and he goes crazy. Then he gives her the pardon for her son, knowing she will burn it. So you see that under that great vision and the ability to change things, this wit, is all the pettiness and narrow-mindedness and in the end destructiveness of the reactionary mind. And his revenge is always malicious.

But this belongs historically more to the eighteenth or nineteenth centuries than to the Restoration. But the play opens in this set-up: we see Lord Are posing in the middle of his country estates, as in a Gainsborough picture.

You are right, but my point was to show society changing. Actually these idiots in the Restoration comedies have the same sort of energy as these men who will invent the railway system, these huge iron bridges – or the biggest ship ever, or tunnels under the Thames, etc. If there is a problem: solve it! Are is developing this energy, this insouciance, this drive that feeds the Industrial Revolution. In the beginning Are is convinced of the power of the feudal world which he can romanticize: even his scarf has to be in the right position in the tree as if the wind blew it there so that he is at home in nature. This is why the play is called 'a pastoral'. But coal is found under his land and he doesn't care to fit in the landscape any more but to turn it into a coal mine. His point throughout the play remains that nothing must change in the class relationships and the respect of the working class for the ruling class. It is a bit like the credo in Lampedusa's *Leopard*: 'Everything must change so that nothing changes.' If it does civilization must come to an end.

Are there echoes of another brilliant and witty upper class, though several generations later, in another character of your historical plays: Mrs Rafi in The Sea? *She lives in a small city on the east coast of England in 1910, and she also uses every means to maintain class rule and order in her community.*

Mrs Rafi is the local Queen Victoria. She isn't puritanical but she is like Voltaire – she doesn't quite believe in God, but wants the servants to. Respectability and conduct of that sort are important to her. Her name is strange. It is a very foreign name for an English person and suggests somebody a bit daring and a bit loose. You have this feeling that, when she was younger, she was different. I think she had an affair with a young Italian poet and they escaped to Italy and he got run over by a horse cart in Turin and then it all came to an end. Then she probably said to herself: 'Well, there you are my girl, if you go on these adventures they end in disaster, so …' So she goes to the other extreme. But she is also a cultivated woman: every so often she would go to London to stay with friends and they would go to modern exhibitions and concerts. She would know about French Impressionism – and wouldn't be totally intolerant of it: 'It is interesting and it is French so it won't catch on here – and if it does we will ban it.' She has experience and she has a wide capacity and vision.

She is also an artist herself: we see her directing the rehearsal of a little show with all these middle-class ladies of the community and the parson. They act and sing some silly pompous and amateurish mythological drama of a bad and mawkish taste.

It is her yearly release. She and the other ladies can act out these bizarre emotions. She overacts and it is terrible – when people begin to escape in fantasies they don't know how ridiculous they become. It is the opposite of the Mummers' Play in *The Fool*. The play is ludicrous and the songs are perfectly grotesque – they do the 'Eton Boating Song', which is an anthem of the most upper-class school in the country – but it doesn't matter as long as it ends by singing: 'There's No Place Like Home', because as she says the town expects it. So they go to hell just to sing this … The play is about Orpheus crossing the Styx to fetch Eurydice – which is really insensitive because they play it in front of a young man who has just been involved in a drowning accident, and has been going to hell, as it were. But this 'play-within-the-play' deals with the same question as the play itself: who will get the girl? A dead ideal hero or can it be an ordinary human being like Willy?

Because the play is about two friends caught in a tempest: one, Colin, the local hero drowns, whereas the other, Willy, survives and will eventually go away from the town with Rose, Colin's ex-fiancée.

Colin is always described by the others as a hero who did everything right, whereas Willy is an ordinary mortal, vulnerable, has doubts and whatever. He has to get rid of these doubts and hesitations in order to go away at the end, but also of all these heroic illusions and accept what reality is. So Willy's journey through the play is a rite of passage towards maturity. The play opens with a storm at sea described as a birth trauma – the storm breaks the sea, as birth is the breaking of the waters – and it ends with two young people who are going to, they hope, change the world. But they are actually going to the First World War that will break out within a few years in which Willy will die, leaving Rose as a widow.

This may be its pessimistic historical horizon but it is not mentioned in the play. It ends on a note of hope.

Yes, but we can already hear the gun battery practising in the open sea over the rehearsal of Mrs Rafi's piece of amateur dramatics. That upsets her very much. It is like reality tapping on the window and saying: 'Yes, but it's all going to end …' The Imperial world, which gives her security, is crumbling – just like the feudal society is breaking down in *Bingo*, or *The Fool*, or *Restoration*. She has to stop the rehearsal. This is what this game I just mentioned with the 'play-within-the-play' is ultimately about: you see the play-within-the-play (Mrs Rafi's) which shows that 'terribly-terribly-terribly sad story' in which the hero (Orpheus) survives but he will not have the girl (Eurydice) because she remains on the wrong bank of the Styx – *she* drowns, as it were, instead of the hero. It is false tragedy ('Isn't it sad?') treated as a comedy. In the *play* (mine), the hero (Colin) drowns and has the girl waiting on the shore (Rose) and she will go to Willy who survived. It should be a comedy. But there is a

WHAT IS TERRIBLE ABOUT IT IS BANAL

further play, a play outside-the-play-within-the-play (history's, played by the guns), which tells how the hero (Willy) who had the girl (Rose) will die in the war in France or in Belgium – and the girl will be left stranded. This is the true tragedy.

It is true Mrs Rafi herself ends the play very depressed after her power has been physically contested: she tried to decently conduct Colin's funeral on a cliff top dominating the sea, but it turned into a farcical row between the ladies in which the ashes are used as missiles.

What happened that day has been so disturbing that the social decorum has broken down and it becomes possible for her to tell the truth and accept her failures. She says: 'I keep everybody in their proper place. I do my Christian duty. I keep order in the community but I'm so bored with them. I have thrown my life away.' Her ability to say that to herself has to be respected and taken seriously: it means to her what she says. She is Hamlet looking at the skull. It has to be as authentic as Lady Macbeth in the candle scene. I once said to an actress who played the part that, after all that comedy, the audience needed to be suddenly taken to the edges of outer space and time. All the artificiality (the bad acting, the false emotion) of the rehearsal scene has to be completely replaced by this and this is what allows her then to tell the truth to young Willy and Rose as they are about to leave the town so that they can be free from the burden of the dead hero. She tells Willy to take Rose away just as Colin would have and to leave Colin's ghost here: 'He's up on these cliffs for ever. A ghost haunting the sea. Till *that* goes – even the sea must go sometime. Even the ghosts.' And she adds: 'Ha, ha.' The whole play is in how to say 'Ha, ha'. It is the most important line in the play – 'Nothing'. You can take the whole Quran and the whole Bible and put it into 'Ha, ha'– if you put it into the situation. Everything in the play is going towards that, it gives you the scale of the whole play. All the murders of the First World War are in 'Ha, ha'. But remember the play is a comedy. Mrs Rafi will stay in this town forever – and soon she will go back down to do her duty and preside over the tea – but Rose and Willy don't need to make her mistake. So, you can see Rafi is capable of self-knowledge, therefore she tends to try to appeal to people's common sense. But when it comes down to the crunch, she is merciless. When Hatch goes mad she says: 'Hatch, pull yourself together', or 'You make it hard for me to help you', but also: 'It would be better if you were to close your shop and leave this town.' She doesn't even have to add: 'You will obey me', because it is obvious he must. She is ruthless.

Hatch is the draper in the community. He has a bizarre paranoid obsession about aliens from outer space, ready to take over the Earth.

Hatch has aspirations. He is like a character from H. G. Wells: the new rising middle class. They become bank clerks and cycle to work – and have clips on their trousers so that they don't get dirty on the bicycle. Some way or another Hatch has been able to get enough money to set himself up in a business, but he couldn't afford to do it in a large town so he settled in this small community by the sea, and he tried to find a place in respectable society. He is very vulnerable and insecure and that is what makes him invent this fantasy about an invasion from outer space. And so *he* is in control, only *he* knows what goes on up there – Rafi and the Parson have no idea, but *he* knows. And obviously Willy is an alien from outer space who came here as a spy. By inventing that he can keep his soul alive. It is his ideology. He is the isolated, deracinated middle class that gets fascistic fantasies.

Like any fascist leader he also drags the local working-class lads into it and they swallow all his stories.

They don't understand all these things but they assume the world is changing ('– They got that thing they call a Zeppelin. It's a ship that can float. – Ships that can float? What nonsense is that?'). Hollarcut has his feet on the ground (which is useful when you're living by the sea), but goes along with it because it is like an adventure that makes his life interesting, and he gets to talk to an educated person such as Hatch, who is the only person who treats him with respect. If you twisted his arm (as Mrs Rafi does at the funeral) and told him: 'Come on, you don't believe all that rubbish, do you?' he'd say: 'Well no, but it pleases Hatch …' He tries to believe it because he is sorry for Hatch.

WHAT IS TERRIBLE ABOUT IT IS BANAL

Hatch stands in between the real and the imaginary, the social classes, the times, the places – because in this unchanging and isolated community he can bring clothes from all the empire and is connected to the capitalist and industrial world outside.

That's why I made him a draper. He has a real intimacy with the fishermen and the farmers but he can be intimate with the ruling-class ladies because they are his customers – but he has to be careful. It would be absolutely impossible for Mrs Rafi to physically touch the draper – and if Hatch has shown the slightest sign of being flirtatious towards her he would have been arrested on the spot. It would have made him a menace to the young ladies. The class relationships rigidly defined English society. They meet in Hatch's shop but he has to keep them apart – and when they actually come together in the same space it is chaos.

This happens during a climax scene where Hatch and Mrs Rafi have a violent row inside the shop that will end up with Hatch physically attacking her.

He just snatches her handbag, but then he has trespassed on a class relationship in a way Mrs Rafi will never allow. Hollarcut is also in the shop – he came to warn Hatch that Mrs Rafi was coming down the road with Mrs Tilehouse and their umbrellas. Hatch is already furious and has in his hands these enormous draper's shears (that will be later referred to as 'murderer's shears') and is quite dangerous and menacing. He actually could accuse Hollarcut of being on her side and attack him with the shears. But when Mrs Rafi comes in, Hollarcut ducks behind the counter where the madman is, rather than being with Mrs Rafi. Imagine Charlie Chaplin who has just committed some offence and is being chased by policemen and finds shelter in a zoo. He can relax and enjoy himself. He sees a lion in a cage, and he starts rattling at it with his stick behind the bar. The lion is getting angry and tries to snatch the stick. Chaplin is really enjoying himself and he looks up and sees the policeman running down towards him. What does he do? He goes into the cage with the lion. The space is concrete in class relationships: you can't trespass on anybody else's space. Hollarcut knows where social reality is, but by the end he has learnt to stand against Mrs Rafi. In the last scene he has the nicest line in the play. Willy patronizes him and says: 'Morning, Billy' and he answers: '*Mister Hollarcut*'. And all Willy says is 'Ah yes' – he sees the world is changing.

The matter of the quarrel is that Hatch has ordered for Mrs Rafi 162 yards of a very expensive blue Utrecht velvet and she refuses to take it – and this refusal would financially ruin Hatch. So he cuts the fabric to force her to take it. He does it so frantically and desperately that he rips and slashes it until he's destroyed all of it.

It is not just an empty rant. Hatch talks about his life as he tears it to bits. He says: 'I walked my life away on this floor. Up and down … Three yards … Why isn't the floor worn … Thirty years … I'm worn through …' He is caught in the ambiguity of his actions. He is ripping the cloth to pieces in order to free himself, but as he is not in control of himself he is destroying it so that it could never be bought and so he is ruined. He is also destroying his relationship with the town. His actions are precisely described and integrate with the spoken text and they should combine and influence each other's meaning. This makes big demands on an actor and is technically difficult to achieve, but the actor can use it to show every thought the draper has had in the last thirty years and the whole meaning of his life. That is the power of acting. Drama can concentrate meaning so that the whole universe seems to lie on one spot. But the cloth is also obviously the sea – as the snow was a sheet of paper for Shakespeare in *Bingo*. So, when he rips it, it is like the storm of the opening scene: the shears flashing around are like lightning, whipping the water and Hatch is drowned in the material. He fights for his life in it just as Colin did when he was drowning and was trying to get out of his jumper in order to be able to swim and save himself.

That is how his body is found on the beach a few days after the storm: the top half of it and his arms are inside in his jumper (as he tried to pull it off) so that its shape is half human, half bundle.

This figure comes from a childhood memory. At the start of the war I was evacuated, like many children in English cities. I was sent to a seaside town in Cornwall. It was as if we went round the universe twice in this train. I was five and I had grown up in London's streets, so to be suddenly presented with something like the sea was very extraordinary. Surprisingly often you could see washed up on the beach bundles which came from refugees' ships that had been bombed and sank. One of them wasn't a bundle of clothes but a drowned man half in and half out of the water. The guy had been fighting to get out of his jumper and he had been washed up with his arms caught in it and his face covered. He died in the act of trying to live. The efforts he was making to live killed him – or if coming out of the sea is a symbol of birth, then the act of being born killed him. It was a very complex image for a child to see. I didn't obviously analyse the image in that way at that time but every evening I would pull my jumper over my head … It is strange in my mind, but to me this story is connected with a precise moment. My sister and I were fostered in a middle-class family which socially was much higher than we were – and to me this was odd too. The man was a professional photographer (but interestingly he never took a photograph of us) and one day he took me to his studio which was upstairs and by the sea – because the light was good. Being up there, feeling I was up at a giant's height, in this light, and looking out at the sea, together with this old-fashioned camera standing on its tripod, I suddenly realized how vast the sea was and all the dreadful things about war became very small. There were very strange elements: photography which is the eye seeing, the beach which could be so very peaceful but which also can be a maniac,and this dead body lying half in the sea and half on the land. It was one of these moments when the world starts asking you questions. It stayed in my mind until I wrote the play in my thirties.

3
LANGUAGE IS AN OCTOPUS WITH A MILLION LEGS

I never write down for young audiences / Young people today take *the present* for granted / Irresponsible adults, children left to themselves: *The Balancing Act* / Adults have absolutely no understanding for the children: *The Children, Eleven Vests* / *Jackets*: the kids do their part very well / The cost of repression on the aristocrats / On the opposite: the two neighbours at the morgue / The language of reality / The profoundest human questions in demotic language / Dominating by language: *The Children, Eleven Vests* / The Headmaster's ritual / From the school yard to the front line / The question of the stranger.

It was some surprise at the beginning, but as a matter of fact you have now written a dozen plays for young audiences since the mid-90s – and you've just written two in the span of one year. Do you find young people easy to contact with your plays?

I was once commissioned to write a play for nine-year-old children. I was a bit scared about it but it actually was very simple: I just asked myself what it was like to be nine years old. It is a formative time in everybody's life so one can remember. It became *Tune*. I saw a performance of it in Birmingham in front of an audience almost entirely of British Asians. They were very young kids, nine and ten, very much under the influence of their parents, with teachers wearing a veil – the girls in headscarves. My play deals with London children in the world I grew up in, so I wondered how could these children understand what it is about. What could I say to them? But the kids immediately owned the play. It is basically about the relationship of trust children have with their parents, so they could identify the various tensions that were shown in the play. They had no problems in relating to it. A girl got very disturbed and had to be taken out – but after the interval she insisted on coming back and following the play through. I was told one of the characters was like someone in her own life – so it was as if the play was written for her. I am constantly told: 'How can a young audience follow all this?' But I answer: 'How could they *not* follow it?' That is the lesson I get from working for young people. They can follow very complicated things because they are not putting into them interpretations that they think are required of them – as adults do. You can actually open for children profound human questions and problems.

Do you have a specific approach when you write this sort of play? Do you force your writing in some way?

I always write my plays for young people to commission, mostly from the Birmingham theatre-in-education company, Big Brum. I have a valuable connexion with them. When I write for them, I have to make sure the technical requirements are not too demanding because they have little money and they move from school to school, so everything has to get in the back of a van. I try to use only one space – or to make changes of venue chaotic and part of the 'scramble' of the play's dynamic. They also only have three actors, which is all the Greek dramatists had (apart from the chorus) – somebody wrote by the way that *The Under Room* was like an Attic tragedy, which is quite fun since the play is set in a cellar … So I concentrate on very few characters and it gives the play a concentration. All this doesn't bring limitations but new strengths. It forces you to concentrate and exploit what you have. It feeds back into the longer plays I write, in a very efficient way. Apart from these material requirements, I have never written children's plays in the conventional sense. I always try to deal with problems they would encounter as adults. And I never write *down* for children.

You even wrote a play not only to be watched by young audiences, but to be acted *by young people – and you significantly called it* The Children *as if* they *were the true subject of the play.*

It was for a working-class school, with no good facilities, in this new estate a few miles up the road from Cambridge University which is incredibly privileged, immensely affluent with these public school boys and girls. The estate children didn't have the help they should have – from the beginning they are selected to be second-class members of society. I approached it not by considering how miserable they were but by wondering what these young people were capable of, what intelligence and energy they had in them. I wrote the text for the two adult actors and I gave the young people only a basic ground text (but carefully written with phrases the children might not normally use) so that they could improvise their own dialogue. Some of the older ones were maybe fourteen but most of them were quite young. It worked very well. There were interesting illuminating incidents. They had a fortnight to work on the play and sometimes I was called in to the rehearsals. The headmaster of the school was interested and made it possible for the young people to rehearse by making it part of the English curriculum. At the end he told me he had been teaching for twenty years and he never knew the kids were capable of this.

Do you find children are very different now from what you were?

Young children now have a different attitude to the future – and this is a crucial point, because human beings began telling stories only because they were conscious there would be a future. Their fathers or grandfathers once would have thought the future would be like the past – perhaps with more aeroplanes, or something like that. But young people today take *the present* for granted (as if supermarkets had always existed), though the ground under their feet is constantly changing. They don't have any conception of the future: it's all 'now, now, now'. The actual practice of modern existence makes life a commodity you are consuming, and you consume it today. There is no point in storing up for tomorrow because tomorrow there would be a new gadget and yours would be rubbish so you would throw it away. I call this a 'binge society': live for today, eat, drink and be merry as if tomorrow you would be dead. Such a statement isn't even a cynical comment on life, it becomes the basis for human existence and it actually takes away your free will from you. At the same time, adults constantly tell them to get educated so that they can find a job in the future. So kids are given two opposed objectives and that explains a lot about 'disruptive youth'. In my plays I want to tell young audiences: 'Think about the future. Where are you going? Tomorrow you won't be dead – with a bit of luck. What you do today is going to build your world tomorrow.' If you take no responsibility for the present – as it is just a question of consumption – you won't have any responsibility for the future: it – the market, authority – decides the future for you. When you deal with young people you are conscious that we are exhausting our cultural capital. It affects language and the meaning of reality as well as how we make ourselves human beings.

In The Balancing Act, *which is a farce, dealing with the possibility of the end of the world, you involve adult characters stupidly boasting about their high cultural standards.*

I recently wrote in an essay about using Shakespeare as a form of high understanding so that people who don't have that sort of education learn to love their ignorance. Young people are often told: 'You are ignorant because you don't understand this.' This is the worst thing for them. The play is making fun of the pretensions of high culture, which is supposed to give a meaning to life and is practically misused by the upper class for repressive reasons. The Foreman in the play, for instance, is a demolition expert who is obsessed with order: everything must be in its proper place, neat and tidy, as if that would solve all his problems. He eventually kills his wife, but he insists on wiping her blood off a knife and getting rid of her body because it would make the place look untidy. Nothing has any real value for him any more – he empties everything of any value, completely. He is not psychopathic: he is the most normal person in the play with a very warm and generous heart and full of goodwill – he speaks Yorkshire and these people are known for their homely and folksy wisdom (about how to deal with 'difficult women' and so on) and also for their phlegmatic way of dealing with disasters: nothing can upset or disturb them. He is not mad – *reality* is mad. The play shows the emptiness of such social behaviour.

This is very much contrasted with the sense of responsibility and the fortitude the young characters demonstrate throughout the play.

There is an image of this towards the end of the play: Nelson, the main character, a very depressed teenager, living rough, enters the Foreman's house in the middle of a farcical, ludicrous situation as if he came from a completely different play – he would be a tragic figure, obsessively collecting and reading these newspapers full of disasters. Originally Nelson would knock on the door and have a conversation on the doorstep ('Can I come in?' etc.). But after seeing a rehearsal, I decided that he would just collapse as soon as the door opens – just crash into the middle of the living room, like a wounded newspaper-seller.

The play opens with this girl, Viv, who locked herself in a house about to be demolished because she believes there lies the spot that holds the world together and she has to look after it so that it is not disturbed.

Children now are conscious that the world is not being well looked after. Some young people are intensely concerned and involved about things they know are happening somewhere in the world and they sometimes feel they can't exist without doing something about it. Perhaps a young mind cannot deal with these things without that degree of seriousness. In the play, Viv has given herself a task, and she is kidding herself that she can solve the problems of the world so easily by guarding the spot. Obviously this is too big a burden of responsibilities put on her shoulders and it destroys her life. But at least she does something. She doesn't give herself the excuse of saying: 'I'm so helpless, what can I do?' At the same time she has this blanket so that she can hide away from reality behind it – for instance, when she is asked to explain what she is doing. Her blanket is part of her inability to deal with the situation – it is like her comfort blanket in a way and she could cover the whole world in it. She wants to face the problem, but she does it in a crazy way. Young people have a lot of sympathy for her. They say: 'Of course she got it wrong, but she is not a crazy girl. *We* can understand her.' The possibility of things breaking down so that the world turns into a wilderness is part of the situation of children now. It is parallel to an emotional emptiness, an emotional loss. That is why in *The Children*, the band of the 'Friends' (who the young audience identify with strongly) go and wander off into a wilderness the adults have deserted. When it happens in the play, children in the audience accept it as obvious. They never ask a question about that.

It is a fact that in this play, and more generally in your plays for young audiences, young characters do have to cope on their own because authority is clearly irresponsible and cannot be relied on.

Kids might feel: 'Yes, but Mum and Dad (or authority, the social services, etc.) would look after it.' And this would be a possible escape for the future. But now their parents are not only killing the children or burning the houses down with bombs, they are preparing a global ecological disaster that is destroying the world. In *The Balancing Act*, I intended to show that the people in authority are not in control – and make it enjoyable, since it is a farce: I show all of them as incompetents, with no alternative to offer. The police are fooled by a one-legged thief, the bus driver cannot drive a bus, the social services woman, a very middle-class do-gooder, hates everybody and eventually, instead of worrying about other people, she decides that all life is about is having holidays in Spain, for which she has developed some romantic refined dreams. And the Foreman eventually picks up on Viv's obsessions for the spot that holds the world and he imagines himself as being the defender of the world and believes it gives him power and control. He is irresponsible and lives on illusions and in the end he gets bored so he just tosses a coin to decide if he will blow up the world. There is an inevitability about the way these people destroy the world.

This stressing of owners of authority as frankly irresponsible seems to me noteworthy for plays supposedly expected to be educational since they address children – and considering relationships with authority is clearly an issue kids are constantly and critically confronted with and have to relate themselves to.

For instance, in *A Window* I deal with drug addiction but it is the mother who takes the drug and not the child, which would be the normal expectation – just as in *Tune* it is the adult who breaks the car window and not the boy. Children who take drugs or destroy things would be a social services problem: authority can come in, pat him or her on the head – or kick his or her backside – and sort it all out. But the real question is not to be at home in your house on the street, but to be at home in the world. I met the same problem when the Berliner Ensemble produced *Olly's Prison*: they insisted on Mike living in a poor neighbourhood – with noise and so on. But it only suggested his problems would be solved if you removed all that – of course it is not true. The point is to make the world a home. By making the authority figures irresponsible, I can open up these deeper questions that cannot be solved by society's usual responses.

It even seems that the very nature of authority consists of being directly hostile to children and even, quite often, openly hateful towards them.

The fact is that children are actually often confronted with quite a strong hatred from the people who are supposed to look after them – though this is not normally publicly admitted, especially when children and adults are together. So I often use in my plays figures suggesting the wicked stepmother in the fairy tales. For instance, in *The Children* there is this Man who has lost his son in the arson of his house. He blames the kids for it, decides they were evil little monsters and he wants revenge on them by killing them all – banging their heads with a brick from his burned house. Towards the end, he first demonstrates being deeply human and then suddenly, in one movement, he swings over to his side and turns into the beast who kills children. The 'Friends' are aware of such hostility even before they have to deal with the Man. They don't run away from home for the adventure but because they know authority, instead of protecting them, will blame them. They actually say: 'Whatever happens now, it will be our fault. Nobody will believe us. There is no way out of this.' The play was partly based on a real incident that happened recently in Liverpool. Two kids about ten had kidnapped and stoned to death a much younger boy. When they were arrested, a mob assaulted the van that was taking them to the police court, screaming: 'Little murderers! Bastards!' They were all adults! I remember one policeman saying about one little boy: 'He's evil.' For me this is no more justifiable than Hitler saying the Jews are sub-humans. The play is not about the murder of the boy but about the attitude of the adults. I also used another cause célèbre of that kind for another play for young audiences, *Eleven Vests*.

The play shows a Student who directly attacks his Headmaster at the school gate and stabs him.

The real event happened in a catholic school in Kilburn. So far as I can remember, the headmaster intervened in a quarrel between pupils involving a knife – he got stabbed and he died. Knife crimes happen often in London but they are usually young people stabbing other young people. Here, it was a figure of authority, so I used the incident to examine the working of authority, which is the play's subject. I am sure the headmaster was as innocent as the young person who killed him. But I remember from a picture I saw that he had in his office a large image of a very graphic and aggressive Crucifixion. It is a very odd image of violence to be put where young people see it constantly. I also remember his wife not saying love your neighbour and so on, but only asking for the penal apparatus to punish the boy. In these two stories, there was absolutely no understanding for the children at all.

More generally, your young characters tend not to rebel against these abusive authorities. The Student stabbing the Headmaster is the only example I see in your plays of a child violently reacting against it.

Such things are part of the difficulties young people have to grow with. Kids know more about violence than most adults, because they tend to be on the receiving end of being knocked about. They can find their ways of responding to it with creativity. I remember for the first production of *The Children*, when we came to rehearse that scene where the Man smashes the head of a boy with a brick, the actor was very cautious with the kid who would play that part. He told him it was just pretending, that he wouldn't hurt him, and told him how he would knock him down, and how he should behave then, and so on. But the kid told him it wouldn't work and he directed the scene with a lot of business and skill and it *was* violent. The kid was clearly used to kids being hit – though not by a brick but by a hand. After that, violence in the play wasn't a problem. Kids can meet disaster and bring their own vivacity to it. I saw during the news about the tsunami in Japan, people being interviewed and saying they lost everything and in the background their kid was at first solemn but then started jumping around making V-signs with both his hands to make fun with the camera. It is not a lack of feeling: children can do the two things. For them tsunamis happen every day: they constantly have to learn resilience in order to cope. Most of the time, they must think the world *is* crazy but they have to integrate with it and get along with it. You have to respond to that strength and that ability. This is why I made *The Balancing Act* a farce: I intended to congratulate, to respond, to recreate the wit and vitality of the young audience. The end is very funny – the kids love it. The world is falling apart and they say: 'Yeah, it serves you right! They deserve what they get!' Laughter is a very serious thing because it allows you to deal with that.

In another play not written for young audiences, Jackets, *you show kids responding with their creativity when they are confronted by the strongest authority: an army. This scene is imitated from a Kabuki play and the situation is that, after a coup, the young son of the deposed Emperor is hidden in a village school. The rebel army, led by General Henba, is searching for him and takes over the playground. There, the children are ordered to parade in front of Henba and each one has to prove he is a real peasant by doing something the Prince could never do – because he is of too high a rank: honk like a pig or bark like a beaten dog and so on.*

These young actors have enormous imaginative power, a great sense of perception, a great sensibility, and artistic creativity which comes from their ability to notice and their need to record. But it is all being corrupted and degraded – just as we were saying earlier on about *The Fool*. You see this creative strength is being used to weaken them because they are induced to behave stupidly – and the danger is that it becomes their normal behaviour. These are things I have heard when I was a child in the Fens: 'Know your place and don't try to get above it because you would be a sitting duck. Play a clown if they want you to because they have that power.' In the play, the village kids are degrading themselves, partly knowingly, and are actually performing the role the aristocrats are giving them as working-class people – and this shows that they regard their peasants as animal. That is in a feudal society where everybody knows their roles and becomes their role. But there, the irony is that the kids can play it *very well* …

Each child is introduced and encouraged by this woman villager, who also comments on what they are doing to Henba.

The woman is like a ringmaster performing in a circus or like a teacher showing the kids how to be more animal-like. She tells them things like: 'Do it worse! Be a real pig: grovel! Be much more like an animal! Show him!' She can see what she is doing and is conscious of the complete situation because she stands in the middle of it and doesn't withdraw from it. She doesn't let the kids damage themselves but she is aware that she is telling them to destroy themselves. She is also commenting on what is happening or is going to happen to the audience of the other villagers offstage. She represents the peasants in front of the aristocrats. The scene is mainly designed to confront the classes with each other and analyse their political relationships. On one side there is this woman and the villagers offstage and on the other side the aristocrats. In between them stands Henba. He is a working-class character who has got power but he despises the people who have power so his sympathy is obviously towards the woman. When a kid comes and claims he is the Prince he can actually respond to this and quite admires him. The aristocrats would have said: 'How dare you say you are the Prince' and they would have chopped his head off for lèse-majesté. Henba treats him like a boy and boxes his ears.

The aristocrats on the other hand are represented by Matsuo. He was the Prince's tutor and he is there to recognize and denounce him when he sees him. But Matsuo secretly remained true to the Emperor and had willingly sent his own son to the village in order to fool the soldiers, who would take him for the Prince because of his aristocratic manners, and kill him and not the Prince. So when he claims he recognizes the Prince, he actually recognizes his own son and sends him to his death.

The aristocrats demonstrate the expected civic decorum and prove their right to rule because they can calculate without being moved by emotion. The scene shows this in an extreme way so that the audience can recognize certain traits of themselves and question the social standards that support them – this is why I used the aesthetics of Kabuki, which is feudal and deeply reactionary drama. But this is a repression of natural responses. Earlier on we saw Matsuo's wife walking alone under the willows wondering, when her son dies, if she will be the proud mother or the mourning mother or the triumphant mother. But she only speculates about these possibilities, because she will do what an aristocrat is meant to do. As she speaks and moves, the actress should push away the (unseen) branches of the willow trees and her gestures should be a sterilized form of the movements inside herself that she doesn't allow herself to feel and represses – as opposed to the big gestures of Hecuba or Cassandra in a Greek play, crying over their fate. Willows are weeping trees and since she can't weep because she is an aristocrat, the willows are weeping for her. You then see that, in order to behave the way they do, the characters had to commit an act of violence on themselves and suppress parts of themselves. That is what lies behind the decorum of aristocracy, this is the cost of repression which dehumanizes them and makes them dangerous.

Later on we will see Matsuo himself staring at the chopped head of his son and showing such an enormous restraint he does not even blink.

This is a very solemn scene (typical of the Kabuki plays) where Matsuo is triumphant because his son has died so well. But a few moments after he viciously screams hysterical abuse at his wife and calls her a whore because she caused a distortion in the ideal performance of duty by his son. He flips from one thing to the opposite. He appears to be in control but he is totally unstable. He becomes more and more dangerous because he would do anything in order to try and recapture control and stick to his training. Normally in people of this sort control is a mixture of sentimentality and malice.

The play has a second part which is set nowadays in a city where the army is about to violently repress a popular uprising. The situation of the aristocratic couple celebrating the sacrifice of their son over his severed head then has a counterpart. We see Mrs Lewis and Mrs Tebham, two neighbours from a working-class area, waiting together at the morgue because the police have found a dead body wearing a jacket belonging to the son of the first woman and require her to identify the body.

Yes, but the scene demonstrates the opposite. Before she is shown the body, Mrs Lewis is fighting for hope that it is not her son. Mrs Tebham exploits the various possibilities opened by their friendship to comfort her and they use their imaginations together to explain what could have happened in the situation and remove the threat. Mrs Lewis is driven by pain and this makes her volatile, so she experiences a whole range of emotions and possibilities, and this leads her to a long self-exploration. This humanizes her and Mrs Lewis in relation to her. In contrast, in the first part, the aristocrats were increasingly dehumanizing themselves: Matsuo was just flipping from one state to the opposite, he wasn't trying to imagine and understand what was happening to him.

The situation takes also another turn because in the scene at the morgue, it turns out that the dead son is not the one they expected. When Mrs Lewis can see the face of the dead body she discovers it is Mrs Tebham's son and not hers. She doesn't tell her but she behaves at the extreme opposite of the Japanese aristocrats: she just bursts into irrepressible laughter!

Indeed, it contrasts with their pathetic pettiness and righteous behaviour – which turns into insulting and abusing each other as soon as they are put under pressure. Mrs Lewis even grabs the shroud from the corpse by accident (almost) – then she covers herself with it in an attempt to protect herself or to hide because she shouldn't in public laugh at the dead – and especially not her friend's son. But you can also imagine she could just rip the sheet off the body and throw it aside and just laugh as if to say: 'I don't bloody care! I want to laugh: I laugh!' This closeness of the tragic and the comic fascinates me. The tragic is so overwhelming and devastating that we could bear it only because we have a sense of the comic – and tragedy purifies the comic and makes it a 'diagram' that allows us to watch it without being destroyed by it. Mrs Lewis is laughing with the profundity of the tragic.

Excuse me, but I really don't see what makes this laughing over her friend's son's dead body better than the restraint of the aristocrats?

The point is not to put a goodie or baddie label on it. In this play laughter, anger, contempt and rage are put in places that seem inappropriate, but it is logic of our life, not convention. Mrs Lewis's laughter is a celebration of the survival of her son. She is showing what drives her to be human, the insistence that makes us human, the human ability to catch the power of life and to give it a cultural role – just like these Japanese kids after the earthquake. Doing this, she really performs an important human truth. She goes on investigating all the different feelings that the situation imposes on her, including her sympathy, so that she recreates herself. So, it is true that she may seem to have no sympathy for her friend, but in this sense, her laughter authenticates more genuinely her sympathy and compassion. It defines reality and the definition then becomes an event in reality. The women try and express the reality of their situation and they are searching for a language that makes it possible for them, they are searching for the language of reality.

What would this 'language of reality' be like?

It is a language from which you could squeeze out the reality of being human, I mean language that allows people to describe exactly *where* they are at *that* moment, what is happening to them in *that* situation, to pin down exactly the situation and the human choices made in that situation. In this scene in *Jackets*, when the women are waiting to see the corpse and are still wondering if it is Mrs Lewis's son, Mrs Tebham eventually manages to provide some miraculous explanations of why there is blood on his jacket without this being evidence of his death – the jacket was stolen, and so on. Mrs Lewis can believe it, it really comforts her and she says: '… O yes. Yes … This is the best one of all.' Then she has the most extreme remark in the play: 'You wipe the blood off the knife even when it's in the wound.' This means that her friend can perform miracles, that she can be so much help. This is a profound remark, it shows real human decency. She reports her experience in a precise statement, a direct literalness – just as she had said just before: 'If you knew 'ow it 'urts', instead of 'Ouch! Uh!' – which possesses its own interpretative authority. She doesn't say merely 'Thanks' because that would only be sentimental. Her description (of the knife and blood) is ultimately political. It means: 'I who say this am able to understand it and I need to say it … and that is miraculous.' She then goes into a reflective speech and now *she* is the one able to create for herself some big elaborated explanations about all that really happened – and Mrs Tebham, who knows this is all fantasies, avoids contradicting her and simply says: 'Yes, something like that.'

Then it is a means for the character to give an account of his current experience?

Not only that. Language has to impose its reality on the situation and at the same time to allow the situation to speak through it. It is not an abstract tool out there, owned by God, or some sort of superior reality – not even owned by grammar because emotion voices itself in language. Language is a human product: it takes on the geography of the outside world and builds an interior structure in the self – but it is also a projection of the human self. In that sense, language is talking for you, it is your own utterance – it is certainly not lacking meaning as postmodernism says – and you have to accept responsibility for it – even if you don't want to hear it. You may ask yourself sometimes: 'Why do I say that?' When you want to say something significant you find one word and immediately after you have others, offering themselves, demanding to be spoken, saying: 'No, it's me! *I'm* the right word!' Language is an octopus with a million legs: whenever you try to grab one you find you are holding another leg. So, language has to change as the characters progress in the knowledge of their conflicts, and they can use it in a more precise and if necessary an even more brutal way. It is important to be conscious that the line, 'You wipe the blood off the knife even when it's in the wound' comes from the same person who said earlier on: 'That dress worries me. It'd cost to have it turned up.' At the end of a scene or a play, someone (or his condition) would be very different than it was at the beginning and he reveals that by his language. It is for language to accomplish the journey between the two ends. Then it becomes the language of reality. That is why language in my plays 'holds' the situations – it is the exact counterpart of the structure. If the language is not there, the situation won't be either.

How do you manage to find this language of reality?

I try to make language speak for itself, be as total as the reality of clothes, if clothes could speak – if only clothes could speak! I don't need to add in surreptitiously the author's comments or an aesthetic awareness so that it becomes something you attend to, reach for – and prove how civilized, beautiful and intelligent you are. I am not commenting on the characters, *they* comment themselves on their

LANGUAGE IS AN OCTOPUS WITH A MILLION LEGS

situation, they speak their democratic truth. I drive them to the limits of their ego and they become open to a sort of 'second world' beyond their consciousness. There is nothing supernatural or mystical in this: it is the world of human understanding, the mundane world, the world of things, when ideological distortions and excuses are removed. It is a world of value and it allows us to act on it. 'You wipe the blood off the knife even when it's in the wound' comes from the world of value. I want to be able to express the ultimate of human experience, in the way that Macbeth can do it, but using the ordinary demotic language that you would use to talk about your laundry or your shopping.

This is an important point to make: all these experiments in language happen within the language of the working class, with its genuine materiality however low or even poor it is in its immediate means.

In my plays, I give these working-class people the parts of the heroes in Greek tragedy. The real analytic ability about themselves and their society goes to them. They have to use language to find and express both emotionally and analytically profound human experiences. So I mean to put the most profound, important and urgent subjects of drama into a demotic intelligence, using a demotic language – which I alter, make sharper, concentrated. This is not a polite academic English, but it doesn't convey any lack of intelligence or insight. It is not a language of stupidity. For instance, when I put country characters in my plays, as in *Restoration* and in the Japanese part of *Jackets* but especially in *The Fool,* I use the dialect from Suffolk which is a very noticeably rural language – without being archaic or the common stage pseudo-rural dialect which is known as 'Mummetshire'. It is the dialect of my grandparents and my aunts who were farm labourers and tended the land. Even after they've been living in London for twenty or thirty years they haven't lost it. I feel at home with it and I like it because it is a very material language in which everything tends to be seen as a metaphor not of the spiritual but of the physical. It has a rhythmic vitality, a curious concrete feel, a harshness. It can be a very subtle and precise language but it is not a language of intellectual ideas in which the logic is sustained by concepts. Instead you sustain it by *pointing* at something: you can have a legal or a theological argument, but the peasant would just point and say, 'look at that'. It is a language which imitates experience. It uses repetitions, like a hammer, knocking, knocking, knocking, but at the same time it can be agile and witty. It has a solid verbal feeling so it can move in the mouth and forces gestures and actions, instead of being just words.

In this respect, Saved *was probably the first opportunity, in a British dramatic culture that still belonged to the upper middle class, to have working-class people appear on stage with all their rights to be themselves, speaking for themselves and as themselves.*

Yes. Most working-class characters were figures of fun – they were comic. In plays by Shaw (who is supposed to be a socialist writer) they are rather patronized or idiots. Committed dramatists often use their working-class characters either to speak propaganda or, in moments of passion, to speak emotionally more intensely. I wanted to create characters who would be at the forefront of experience and so they would necessarily have to be working-class because other classes depend on ideological lies or are struggling to get out of them. In any case that was my background – this language came naturally to me. I put it in situations I knew because they were situations I grew up in. *Saved* didn't show anybody who wasn't a member of the working class. It would have been easy to introduce, say, a probation officer or a priest who would belong to the middle class at least in his philosophy. The people in *Saved* are funny, witty, sharp – though they were expected to be grunting animals. But like the pupils in the school village in *Jackets*, they are observant, bright and precise. Whenever they meet outside authority it is described mostly in terms of satirical humour or sometimes in anger – but their humour is most often turned against either themselves or against each other.

In your plays, language is also a means for authority to demonstrate itself. It can even stand itself as an authority. For instance, this is how the Headmaster in Eleven Vests *tries to dominate the Student: by deploying huge quantities of language. For the first half of the play the Student doesn't say a word but he has to endure these extremely long and uninterrupted inquisitive speeches.*

Because the Headmaster is authority, he is articulate, and he is able to use language in a manipulative way, combining threat with self-pity, emotions and fear. He says things like: 'I devoted my life to pupils. I'm only doing it for the best. I want your wellbeing more than you do. It hurts me more than it hurts you. Please help me.' This is verbal violence: it destroys any possible human relationship between them. The Headmaster can stop this at any time if he tried to understand the Student instead of insisting the Student understands him. If the Student had answered: 'I am so sorry and you are such a nice person', it would have corrupted him. Whatever his answers, it would have been corruptive because the Headmaster could have coped with it, known which slot to put them in – they would lead to the Student's corruption and added to the Headmaster's corruption. The Student is the victim of the prison the Headmaster is in.

This also happens to Joe, the main character of The Children*, with his mother who relentlessly tries to talk him into committing arson for their sake.*

She is a very disturbed woman and she manipulates her boy terribly through this long speech. For instance, she demands that he agrees to do something *before* she says what it is, because she says this would prove he loves her – so in the end Joe is begging to be told what it is. Or she says she would do it herself, but she can't for his sake because she would be put into prison so he would lose his mummy, etc. Not all mothers actually ask their kids to burn down houses but they do have ways of manipulating them. This is the idea of St Augustin: 'Love and then you can do what you like.' By the way, it is a strange experience for an actress to talk to a child-actor and not get the normal responses of an adult actor. It is very powerful to watch. The simplicity of the child's silence gives him as an actor enormous power in the scene. The Mother or the Headmaster have to work against the child's remoteness from them and the more they talk, the weaker they become.

Instead of speaking, the Student in Eleven Vests *vandalizes a school book, then a school uniform jacket of his friend, before, as we saw earlier, directly confronting the Head.*

The book is a source as well as an icon of knowledge. The Student destroys this because it doesn't give him knowledge in the right way.

You know in England school uniforms have a badge on the jacket. It is not just the name of the school. I went to a basic working-class school where we learnt only the most elementary things but we had on our school crest the Latin motto: *Sursum Corda*. The badges are just fake heraldic images but they come out of centuries of history and they go right on your chest over the heart: BANG! So when the Student in the play destroys the jacket he attacks the school and its regimentation, not only the knowledge but the school as an institution. Then you can see the anger coming from the object to the person. He wouldn't at first attack the schoolmaster directly: he mediates the direction of his blow through the jacket of another pupil. The Student is really saying to the Headmaster: 'I destroyed the book, did you get the message?' No. So he destroys the jacket: 'Did you get the message?' No. So he goes on and attacks the teacher. 'Did you get the message now?' The message should have been learnt when he destroyed the book. The people yelling revenge on children in the real incident didn't get the message either. All the Headmaster is doing is giving him a lesson in authority and administration – whereas the student tries to send a message in justice. Why does he remain silent, then? Why did Christ remain silent at his trial?

This fatal confrontation occurs at the school gates. The Student had been expelled but he tries to come inside, and the Head forbids him to. Eventually, and still silently, he stabs the Head – who kept speaking constantly.

Authority flips at that moment. Normally it compels children to come to school but when it comes to a situation it cannot handle, it forbids them to come. The Student didn't come back with the intention of killing, but to confront the Headmaster – he might have only shown him the knife. It is sad that he has to go back to the school. It is as if he still needed school to understand him. He would need to ask why he has to come back to the school, but to articulate this would require self-knowledge and he is not allowed in this situation to have it. He just doesn't have the language for that. The Headmaster cannot teach him this language because he is only lying to himself. You often hear parents say: 'My kids don't talk to me', but they haven't given them a language with which they can first speak to themselves in silence. We don't have a language that allows us to tell the truth any more, that can relate us to the world in a useful way.

After he stabbed the Headmaster, instead of running away he stays there and makes one step through the gate.

But first he throws the knife as evidence, as if to say: 'This is it, I've done it. I want to leave my mark here.' Stabbing the Headmaster is killing authority, breaking the rules. So crossing the barrier of the gate with his foot is a demonstration of freedom. It is as if he had stabbed the school, the community, its world. That is the Student's total confrontation. There is also an unseen chorus of students at the windows of the school watching what is going on. At that moment they all scream, because they are not used to freedom and are frightened by it now that the authority figure has been removed. That is a common experience with my plays: people get upset because I present them with freedom. But at some performances by Big Brum, when the Head got stabbed, the students in the audience cheered …

The second half of the play moves to a different set-up. The Student has become a soldier and we see him on the front line. It is only then that we hear him speak.

Yes, but in the meantime we have seen him as a novice recruit being trained to bayonet his enemy – a sack stuffed with straw. He then produced sounds that are meant to copy the screams made by the Instructor: 'Ha! Ha!' Once again his silence contrasts with a long speech. The Instructor holding a rifle first speaks very rationally of technology and civilization and then, after he puts a bayonet on the rifle, he abruptly turns into a maniac and screams and shouts orders to kill kill kill. This language shows that the Instructor can hold two different strata in his psyche, a 'rational' and a 'maniac', each of which simplified the other so that he can easily go from one to the other. It is as if he were the Head with his articulated language but now armed with a bayonet. In this scene, the book and the jacket have become a sack stuffed with straw, and it is now legitimate to stab it – and the Student is even *ordered* to do so. He is now exposed to the contradictions which were concealed in the school scenes. It is as if the whole society was contained in the action of stabbing. This is the state of social contradiction of most of the young people who are the audience of the play.

Once on the front line, the Student finds himself in the situation to put into practice what we saw him learning. He captures an enemy squad but he is shot at and his fellow Soldier is killed by an Enemy who didn't know his mates had surrendered. So the Student decides to bayonet him.

There, the book/jacket/sack becomes a person. In the beginning the Student attacked a book with his knife because he considered knowledge as corrupt. Now the Student appears as a soldier with a helmet and a gun with a bayonet – and earlier on we heard the Instructor describing the gun as the sum of all human technological civilized knowledge. In front of him is the Enemy kneeling and imploring him. So you see the contrast between corrupt and destructive knowledge and the naked human being who asks a question.

This question is for the Student because the Enemy speaks to him in his own language which the Student can't understand.

The Enemy can't communicate with him and explain how he came to shoot at him by mistake. So he is put into the situation of the Student in the first scenes when he didn't have the language to be able to enter into a discussion with the Headmaster and state his own point of view. The only way left to the Student to communicate with authority was to stab the Headmaster. He committed an act of revenge against authority. Now he kills someone who is a foreigner but who is like himself. Both are victims in relation to authority.

The Enemy dies repeating for the Student in his own language a sentence the Student will never know the meaning of – neither does the audience. What does he say?

I really and deliberately don't know! It is just random typing really: 'Vczxq Nabczxsd. Vzcxadsf.' I used this language again for another foreign character in *The Under Room* so it became a 'Big Brum language'. People in the audience ask me what the Enemy says but

I want the audience to ask itself that question. I don't want them to understand the play, I want them to understand themselves. What happens becomes an enigma because the Enemy does something very inappropriate.

Actually, after he has been bayoneted, the Enemy, presumably dying, has this amazing gesture: he sits up and uses his vest to try to wipe his own blood from the bayonet.

This takes away the screens and opens up reality. At the end of the bayoneting lesson the Student received the order to clean the scattered straw with a broom – every scrap of it. You can understand the meaning of this order (and the empty clear space, as if nothing has happened there) but what can this other gesture of cleaning the bayonet that killed you tell you about order? The Enemy must take care to try and get rid of the blood so that there has never been blood, never been war … It mustn't be easy to do (not as if he just came back from the dead to say that it is wrong to bayonet people) and it should be long enough for the audience to ask themselves what is happening. What he says is: 'Understand me! Understand this! Look what you've done!' The Student is caught by this enigmatic gesture and sentence. He asks another enemy soldier to translate but what he is really asking is: 'Why didn't he just lie there dead? Why didn't he say: "Please?" Or: "You bastard!" Why does he want to do that?' Actually the Student is asking himself the question of the Headmaster in the first scenes. He was then unable to answer in a useful way for himself but now, at the end of the play, he has come through a series of experiences so that ultimately he can think and gain some knowledge about himself and his situation. The dying Enemy is asking him to live his life for him. Perhaps that is the meaning of humanness: we must learn to live other people's lives. Then at last we shall have our own language. It is the language only drama can teach us.

4
IN ALL THESE GAPS THERE IS THE POSSIBILITY OF FREEDOM

Saved: mending a chair in silence / Something of Hamlet, a guy asking questions / The attack in the park: a matter of escalation and positions / An act of justice from society / *The Tin Can People*: Affluence can't be a sufficient grounding for humanness / *Olly's Prison*: Western capitalist society is empty / 'A lad just left' / The questions of King Lear in a tea cup / Frank, a very destructive policeman.

You showed another kind of impossible communication, without any foreign language being involved, in the last scene of Saved. *The whole play is about a working-class family of three, in which nobody gets along with each other – the parents don't even talk to each other and they even physically fight. At the end you just show them during an almost mute scene, sitting in their living-room silently going about their own business and ignoring each other.*

The silence in the scene is like the silence of the tomb. This silence always disturbs directors: they always want to add some music or sound or whatever to fill it. The mother and father never talk to each other and you could now feel these people have nothing to say to anybody any more. They would have obvious things to say to each other but they don't have the words. They are condemned to silence.

They are driven to an even further state than these 'couch potatoes' who stay at home staring at the television and all the rubbish that comes through it: they sit in their room, and they don't even bother to turn the television on. Their inability to understand, or even to listen to each other, drives them into comatose silence.

But into this family has come a young man, Len, who had an affair with the daughter, Pam (and possibly got her pregnant) and stays in their home whatever the hardships.

Len seems to have dropped from outer space. In scene one, he comes like a stranger into the room (and it isn't the room he expected) and then he is slowly enclosed into the problems of the house – which are the problems of his society. They all need Len for their own motives but they have no way of explaining this, no way of communicating to each other. They just cling to him as a lifebelt on a sinking ship, even Pam.

But Pam keeps rejecting Len. She hangs on to the local tough guy, Fred, claiming he made her pregnant, though he *rejects* her *more and more violently.*

Pam is cluttered up by her family life and this shadows her attempts to escape. She has never asked her parents why they are enemies – or if she has, she soon learnt not to – so she just bears their wound. Pam has no concepts to fall back on – only desire. She is a vacuum with a desire – and her desire can't be fulfilled. Her parents have not loved her and have given her no purpose in life. She desires what her parents could not give her so she can only be content with someone who doesn't want her – and as that can't give her contentment she can never be content. So she can't bear Len *not* rejecting her. She drops him and disregards his feelings and presence and 'goes for' Fred, who absolutely refuses to have anything to do with her, because this repeats her psychological drug. Her life is about being rejected and the only way she can live is by being rejected. She has nowhere 'out' to escape to because she would bring her desire with her. Len knows that situation is unliveable but he decides to stay, not because he is trapped and he can't get out, like Pam, but as a common acceptance:

IN ALL THESE GAPS THERE IS THE POSSIBILITY OF FREEDOM

'Don't run away from the scene of the accident, don't pass by on the other side.'

Len is present in this last silent scene, and he is the only one who actually does something: he mends a chair that had been destroyed in a violent row between the parents in a previous scene.

In this situation Len knows somewhere that the family is broken and that he has to repair it as well as his own life. He doesn't know how – but he knows how to repair a chair – so he does and this becomes an exercise in creating. And nobody cooperates – he only asks Pam once for a hammer. Is he defeated and nails the nails for his own coffin? Or will this experience bring him closer to his own creativity, to his own humanness? Instead of verbalizing, I wanted to show him physically shaped by that activity of repairing the chair so you can then see the human effort that goes through reproducing society. I have taken his poses from statues of Michelangelo – not one in particular, but their plastic sense, the arrested human movement they show that allows you to see the tensions within movement, how the aim is arrived at.

What makes Len different from the others?

Len is more perceptive or more concerned (or more worried) than other people and so is able to articulate, or to show, more about their situation. It is his nature to question himself: 'Why does this happen? Why do I think that?' He has the purity of the questioner. I often do this in my plays: I concentrate on somebody who is able to ask more questions than other people, but who remains a member of the group. John Clare, for example, or Scopey in *The Pope's Wedding*, who has the ability to be the hero as well as the social outcast, or more recently Luke in *Born*. He is a member of a killing squad, he has been trained to perform violence and has the same orders to kill as the others, but he wonders what it is like at that moment when you know you are going to die – and he wants to know from the people he kills. The question behind this is: 'What is the meaning of life?' So he believes that only his victim can tell the meaning of what he, the aggressor, is doing. He has something of Hamlet: a guy asking questions. He becomes a figure of the quest: he cannot prevent himself from asking his question because he is obsessed by it, possessed by it. It drives him further and further, he notices more and more things, and becomes more and more involved in the question. Because he pursues this question, he eventually meets something human inside it, something of the human reality. In these characters, such as Len, I show the strength that is aborted and wasted in other characters and this creates difficulties for them. The tragic irony is that Len is in some way their answer and so they need him.

Does this mean the others don't question their situation?

The others have learnt that questions are disturbing things, are unsettling, so you don't ask questions – and perhaps you don't talk – or not to people who would ask you questions. This community requires conformity because it is policing itself. Being daring and anarchic can be a virtue as long as it remains within the conformity of the group. The people we see in the play want conformity because nonconformity becomes a question. So Len is pushed away when he asks too many questions. He would not accept what things are. Fred tells him this straightforwardly when they have their long discussion in the park by the river: they talk about their lives and jobs, their situation in general, and Fred says he has to integrate more into the group and that his trouble is that he keeps asking questions: 'Why don't you shut up and fish and get the girl? Just be! Stop wondering about all these problems.' But at that moment Pam comes on with the baby claiming it is Fred's. She presents him with a big problem. His situation is questioning him. So this 'stop asking questions' is not true: Fred is full of questions. He is not what he poses as. Until then Fred was the nice guy, Jack-the-Lad, and suddenly he is asked to be responsible for his own actions. Then he becomes very angry and very violent with Pam so that she ends up leaving the baby for him to take care of and Len goes off after her to bring her back.

So, here we are at this famous scene when the baby is attacked and stoned to death in his pram by Fred and the gang – the scene that brought you fame, blame, infamy, censorship ... You were accused of showing and indulging barbarians behaving like animals.

They are not beasts nor are they seeking for opportunities to be beasts – they are searching for their humanness. I wanted to make clear that these people were very dissatisfied with themselves. I thought the play would be useful if the audience could understand their situation because I meant to draw attention to – and use the tensions between – the things that were wrong in our society as a collective. I think the play speaks for itself to any honest person who can speak to himself or herself honestly. The critics wanted me to create cretins instead of people in trouble, who are confused and do not understand their situation. When I wrote that scene (more than fifty years ago now) I didn't have any theoretical understanding myself. I was just responding to the reality of those people in that situation: What would they do? How would they behave? What sound would they make? What does the situation do to them? I tried only after to understand it and talk about it. All I wanted to do was show a fact of our society. Shakespeare didn't have a theory about witches – where do they come from? Who are they? He just accepted it as a fact of his society – they burnt witches, didn't they? Anyway, in my plays the violence tends to be very limited, especially compared to television. It is noticed because it doesn't occur in the conventionalized acceptable way.

Let's leave this polemical ground and have a closer look at the scene itself to see how it proceeds. So this baby-question is left there, on his own, in the pram.

… and Fred's gang comes in. They are going out for the night, 'up West' – that means the West End where there are bars and girls and which is a much more affluent area where they are not really at home. It is like going to Disneyland: they escape from their world and enjoy themselves. So one of them wears a new jacket. The scene is very carefully structured. It is essential to get the setting and the timing right because it is a matter of escalation as much as a matter of positions: the gang is there, but Fred is just sitting there downstage, apart from the others in silence, totally absorbed in his own problem and for a long time he doesn't get involved in what happens behind him. The gang has this series of games beginning with the cigarette on the ground that leads them to the pram. The baby is not yet an enemy but only an element of their games that gives them an opportunity to laugh at Fred's fatherhood. But then the situation is asking them questions too because the baby is in the wrong place doing the wrong thing.

The baby is not reacting because Pam has stuffed it with aspirins to stop it crying. So they begin to tease it and to play with the pram to wake it up for fun. But their vocabulary and humour is already very violent and macabre.

The baby is there like a huge unanswered question and they try to integrate it in a situation they can control. That of course exposes the fractures inside the community, what they are apprehensive about, what they cover up, what they try to put together: they show how they survive in that situation. First they talk about reassuring the baby, then about how society controls its victims (punishing, racism, and so on …). It is just a question of controlling the situation and retaining the group's cohesion and this comes down to solidarity and shared recognition. That challenges Fred and brings him back into the group because he has been dealing with the same kind of problem that the gang had: How do you survive in this society? Their games go on until the new jacket gets ruined because one of them rolls the pram over it. If it hadn't been for this jacket, the baby wouldn't have been killed. Everything escalates from there and the fighting for fun becomes serious then because clothes are expensive and concern virility, which in the group is social power. Then the games with the pram turn into a conflict.

They begin to push the pram at each other, more and more aggressively.

It is only then that someone really looks at the baby. And what does he see? Something helpless and insignificant, dirty, neglected, drugged, and probably terrified, even in its sleep – or is it too shocked to respond? They are all stuck because they see themselves – precisely themselves – in the same condition as the baby. The concentration on the baby's little fingers suddenly reveals vulnerability and it becomes the centre of their world. This is a special step forward in the scene after the almost comic bravado, into a dangerous slope. I remember during a rehearsal of the play in Alfortville (a working-class Paris suburb) I set an exercise in which the actors had to specifically observe the baby; then I repeatedly asked them what they saw in the pram. It went on for a very long time. Then one of them finally answered: '*C'est moi*' – 'Myself'. They were all trying to be boss and suddenly they are presented with

IN ALL THESE GAPS THERE IS THE POSSIBILITY OF FREEDOM

this image telling them: 'Actually, you are like me: you are as helpless and have as little control over your life as this infant in the pram.' It is the opposite of Snow White's magic mirror; instead of saying: 'Yes: you are the great man, and you don't care what anybody thinks about you as long as they know you are the boss – or as you are in the community where we all support each other', suddenly the mirror says: 'You are shit.' Obviously they don't like what they see and they start smashing the mirror in rage ('It's not true! I'm not like that!'). Their anger is a revenge against themselves – and it is stronger than any aggression against the others. Ultimately the desire, the rage, for revenge is to see your own dead body. If we could see our own dead body we would immediately become human. So, you see it is not a question of people being beasts. Basically people work on two motives. One is innocence: they want to be at home in the world. The other is revenge: when innocence is denied it turns into corruption – then you take revenge and destroy innocence and justice. Ideology exists on the cusp between justice and revenge.

Then they start really tormenting the baby itself fiercely: pulling its hair, pinching it, punching it, spitting at it.

It may seem that the men don't know what they are doing – but they do. They soon know they are harming the baby and when Fred joins them in throwing the stones they know they are killing it. All this happens because the baby looked at them innocently. They could see innocence looking at them, seeing *through* them and they couldn't bear that. They are not naturally cruel. The cruelty is only incidental in that situation, it is what society offers to survive. Fred and the others in the gang are the neonate made barbarous. I put somewhere in the scene the direction 'groaning' to suggest the awakening of an inside pain which is normally hidden by the laughter of the gang. When they leave, they make a 'curious buzzing', like bees getting nervous inside a beehive, or the water in a kettle close to boiling – it should be as quiet as that. Really the gang don't make the noise. It is the tension in the theatre *felt* by the audience. These noises are the gang's own pain and as they can't express it their rage is intense and the attack on the baby deadly. The situation runs out of control, until the stones come. The stones bring a moral ambiguity: brave David killed tyrant Goliath with a stone, and good people used to stone the criminals in biblical times. This is what really disturbs the audience: the moralist always has a stone in the hand. But the stoning in the play is the process by which the victims become the torturers. It is an act of revenge society needs in order to maintain injustice.

How can you involve society as a participant in that murder? The boys are clearly on their own on the stage, there is no pressure from any authority.

The baby is killed because society is corrupt. How could an innocent survive in an unjust society? Society creates huge reservoirs of violence by injustice and then represses it by ideology and by bribery. The stoning is an act of justice against the injustice of society. It is the individual destroying himself out of rage against the violence society is using to repress him. I show what is in this logic of personal aggression. That is – in terms of dramatic irony – a creative use of violence by the characters themselves. The scene is revelatory because in it society tells itself the truth. For the audience it invokes the moral ambiguity in the use society makes of violence. The stoning opens the drama of innocence. The young men kill the baby out of the nostalgia to be human.

We will later know that Len, who is offstage, is observing the scene from a tree; he sees everything but he doesn't intervene either.

Yes, you would think that the spring of human kindness and compassion would surely work in him if he is the goodie-goodie and he would have jumped down from the tree and rushed over and said: 'Stop! Stop! You mustn't do this! It's inhuman!' He would have if he had an answer and what stops him is the question – really it is as simple as that. I could have made him absent but I wanted him to learn more about his situation. He is being asked by the situation what is the meaning (or the value, or the purpose, or the responsibility) of life. Later he asks Fred what it was like when he killed the baby.

IN ALL THESE GAPS THERE IS THE POSSIBILITY OF FREEDOM

Could anything have stopped this escalation towards murder?

It just needed one of them to say: 'Wait a minute. What are we doing?' The scene is like an obstacle race: the guys have to cross a new obstacle each time – but they can refuse each one. For this it needed a society which has questions – we don't. We just have answers. That is why our culture becomes a form of repression instead of being an insight and a means of creating freedom by enabling you to question the contradiction and the restrictions you are in. The present Prime Minister talks about ours being a broken society, but we are broken by society's answers – answers he would regard as successes: commercial ability to provide consumer goods; the world of things. I have already said that once the working class was controlled by deference, nowadays it is patronized and given more consumer products as a solution to its dissatisfaction. Modern capitalism doesn't want deference. It wants people not only to know their place but to aspire to get out of that place, and it deceives them into achieving this by consumption. Consuming is the great answer but it doesn't answer the human question. People are unable to be in control of their life and so are incapable of happiness and they become like drug addicts addicted to consuming.

Your play The Tin Can People *provides a powerful image of this. It is about a small community (that gives its title to the play) of survivors after a total nuclear war, who have found virtually infinite army storehouses with millions of tins that can feed them for generations.*

They are in what should be a paradise. They seem to be given everything: they have plenty of food, living space and buildings, they don't fear hunger or poverty, they do not need to labour to earn a living, there is no need for exploitation, they are not threatened with the nuclear holocaust (they have survived it) so they needn't act out of fear of the future, or struggle for their freedom and their rights. This should answer all their questions but it doesn't. Western capitalist consumers' democracy isn't the end of history or the answer to the human riddle. Affluence can't be a sufficient grounding for humanness because it cannot solve the human ambiguity. This dramatizes our vision of utopia (which I think is unrealistic) and shows it remains a form of prison.

Why doesn't it work for these 'tin can people'?

They don't have to practically produce their lives so they have no practical relationship with the world. When they are confronted with a practicality, that is a stranger carrying a disease that could kill them all, they panic, become irrational and destructive – like all ruling classes faced with the non-economic problems of life. You can't just stand in such a situation where everything is so perfect that the other considerations just vanish – because reality in itself is not just. The presence of the stranger is fatal and destructive because it brings them reality (death) and they cannot control this. It is not that the man brings them a disease: the disease is in them and all he does is point at this disease. It is their fear of him that destroys them.

In their fury they destroy all their stocks and at the end of the play you show them ready for a new beginning where they themselves will have to make their means of surviving.

They got rid of their answer and this confronts them with new questions on which they could build themselves. Now they have to ask themselves what to do, and take responsibility for their answers and the actions they will accomplish on these.

You also show this consumption as an answer given by society to people's unasked questions in a more mundane situation in Olly's Prison. *We see Vera's apartment which you write is 'overcrowded' by furniture and ornaments, the triviality of which 'makes it seem empty'.*

Nowadays commodities signal emptiness, they don't have real human purpose any more and people surround themselves with things that don't really give sense to their existence. This doesn't create social happiness. All the decoration Vera puts into her room doesn't humanize it, it just fills it with rubbish – just as most of the time all she wants from her friend Mike are tokens: 'We're together, aren't we? We're sharing our life, aren't we?', but not any real sharing. Vera would settle for a certain routine, stop asking the ultimate questions and be sufficiently happy about that – as I said about Fred in *Saved*. Modern Western capitalist society is empty. In this play, Olly (the character of the title)

IN ALL THESE GAPS THERE IS THE POSSIBILITY OF FREEDOM 81

keeps signalling emptiness with his gestures – like a kid signing he has got a pain. He makes the gesture 'Hi!' like an Indian chief, not as a friendly wave but just to show an empty hand. He then mimes shaking hands at a distance and later on he sits and tosses his shoes behind the armchair and creates the absence of the space behind the chair, or takes a vase and not only looks inside, but turns it upside down, as if he could empty emptiness out of it, like water, so that he can authenticate, stress the bleakness of his life. He uses the vase to show the emptiness that he feels his life and everybody's is full of. His name is derived from the element of a matchstick man: O for the head, an inverted Y for the trunk and legs, and two Ls stuck on the trunk for the arms – the modern Everyman: the 'O' is a hole. It fits into the running visual schemes in the play of containers, cupboards, cases … and prisons. The characters are frequently surrounded and put into contact with things that are empty. The play opens with Mike sneezing offstage, as an echo of emptiness from someone who is not there. The cupboard where later on Mike will try to hang himself contains empty buckets, pipes and so on. Cupboards are spaces of emotional emptiness – just like Vera's rooms and the prison cells. After he finds a prison mate, Smiler, hanging in this cupboard, Mike has a moment of extreme emptiness and hides *under* his bed, as if the space under his bed was an empty container. The play puts the audience in the emptiness.

How are the characters affected by this emptiness that the play points at in their life?

Look at Mike's situation at the beginning of the play: he is imprisoned in routine and the structure of authority, everything has to be in its proper place, and has to have a proper explanation and reason. He has a job but he is fascinated by a lad, a younger man who has 'just left' work that day, without planning for a future. He didn't want the wage slavery and decided to walk away. Mike has a long opening monologue, speaking to his daughter, and he returns to the lad at crucial moments – but it needn't be played as an obsession. He sees it as an arbitrary act he can't understand because he thinks you only leave your job when you have another job to go to. But he also sees it as a sudden dash for freedom. When he was young he had himself once toyed with the idea of making such an escape, to Australia (the upside-down land), but he met his wife and he stayed trapped, in prison. He says to himself: 'This guy has chosen freedom and I'm caught up in this business. I'm a slave of modern industry.' He is actually facing his own death. I suppose he could smile, watch the telly, read the newspapers, but a voice in him would be saying distinctly: 'You're dead, aren't you? You are wasting your life. You won't have another chance.' The lad 'just leaving' opens a series of sudden unexplainable events, which are the basic units of the play's structure, constantly repeated in different forms and that open as many 'gaps' in reality. A gap is what can't be explained any more by usual answers – ideological and superstitious false meanings. There is no laid-down route in the gap, the characters just don't know where they are. They have to ask why. So the gap is where meaning must be created: either humanness or corruption. The gap lurks everywhere but it is not just some waste bin you can put anything in. The gap is what allows you to imagine and its only real part is the imagination and its logic. You put in what you imagine and this defines what you are as a human being. When people (characters or audiences) try to avoid questions and meaning, they try to fill the gap with habits, routine, possessions, and this leads to disasters. In their paradise, the Tin Can People had, in theory, filled the gap with the tins. At the end, when they destroy their tins, they recreate the gap and that is the foundation of humanness for them. *Olly's Prison* confronts the characters with a series of strange happenings which are like signposts to the gap. The first one is the lad's choice of freedom and it is a sign that in all these gaps there is the possibility of freedom. It is there that Mike goes in order to find meaning.

Mike is also immediately faced with another question: his daughter, Sheila, sits there at the table, and she won't drink the tea he made for her or say a word to him or even move and give the slightest sign of hearing or caring. This turns into a confrontation that will end with Mike strangling her to death. Why does this incident become so big?

The sudden remembrance of freedom had disturbed Mike and now his daughter disturbs the home routine by not being able to talk to him or to drink her tea. It is one of those small things that make you get desperate and desperate and desperate. They can take you over. The scene must begin casually, politely and quietly for the actor to slowly trap himself. If he immediately rows there won't be a problem: he would go out and get drunk, or yell at his daughter and exhaust his anger before they are at real risk. The time bomb lies within their situation and so in their psyches. Mike gets some assurance that he is not wasting his life, because he is looking after his daughter. That would give him a handrail – just as decorating her flat does for Vera. He is not dead because he can make her a cup of tea. It is a human gesture, on the most profound subjective level: to be alive for a human being means to be able to share your life, to make contact with somebody, to share somebody else's humanity. Mike is asking for only one gesture of human solidarity. He believes if she drinks her tea, picks up the cup, using her hand to make a human gesture that will show what is in her mind, then it would mean he is in a world of human purpose. It will not solve all his problems but he won't be in a madhouse: cause and effect will make sense, the universe would be in focus, it would become a site where we can live. Halfway through he says: 'It's not a cup a tea any more. Gone beyond that.' It is much more important now and they can't escape from this. Mike wants to know ultimately if the universe is a human place. Is it a place where he can find his isolated self? Can he share it with other human beings? Or is it just a padded cell? But she won't do it because for her the teacup is empty – for her his gesture of giving her the tea is not a fully humanizing gesture. And that ends in chaos.

The murder comes quite unexpectedly but during this long monologue (it lasts some forty minutes in performance) Mike is led by an insistence in questioning his daughter's unexplained silence and it is clearly his question that drives him to murdering her.

As Mike talks, the nature of what he is saying becomes more and more abstract or generalized and at the same time more personal and basic. He keeps repeating: 'Drink the tea! Drink the tea!' But he is also asking himself: 'Why do I want her to drink the tea?' He examines all the possibilities to force or convince her to drink her tea, using the table and the cup – like a child would play with a toy tea set to understand how adults live. And in doing so he tries to find why he is there and demonstrates all the complications and compromises you have to make in order to exist. He comes to ask basic ontological questions, dealing with human value: 'Do we love each other? Can we respect each other? What is the point of freedom?' – the questions of King Lear, Prince Hamlet, the most profound questions a human being can ask – and they all come down to his kitchen table in his little flat in a block in the London suburbs. The energy of the scene will come from its specific quiet as the actor slowly unwraps a map of the world, broadening his questions and reflections on the past, the future, the dead and the living, and to neighbours and strangers, until he opens it out to the hole under his feet. A cup of tea. This must be an experience of vertigo not only for Mike, but for the audience. Living in a society like ours is like living on a tightrope: a lot of things keep you balanced but there is a huge gap beneath your feet. My plays intend to disturb the social balances between things so that you become aware of that gap. Sometimes my scenes can have an explosive effect not because I have splashed the stage with blood or something but because they open a space, open a gap. That is frightening but if you can follow what is happening, so that it becomes creative logic for you, then that produces a great feeling of freedom. That is *very* different from most of the left-wing political theatre which usually wants to tell the audience how bad this or that is. I want *the audience* to tell how bad it is and ask themselves: 'What am I doing on this tightrope over this abyss?'

Mike's crime is dealt with by the law which doesn't ask why but puts him in jail, where we see him at length in the play. One of the inmates is Smiler, who is a prominent figure; he is a young guy, very vivid, but the night before he is due to be released he hangs himself in a noose Mike had prepared for himself. This unexplained suicide then adds another question for him and the other characters.

For everybody Sheila and Smiler were the enigma: Why was Sheila silent? Why did Smiler kill himself? Everyone in this play obsessively seeks the meaning of their and the others' actions – like people falling who both seek and fear the ground rising up under their feet. They almost *feel* the gap as the presence of a space which they cannot easily enter. They never talk about it metaphysically but always in simple terms of objects and situation. When Vera can't understand what Mike does she just asks him: 'Tell me about the other things.' She means the mystery her pathetic possessions cannot explain. In prison Smiler says to another inmate it is no use telling him what he will do when he goes outside because the other inmate wouldn't understand – and I suppose that Sheila in the first scene (if she ever listened) was telling herself: 'What's the use of me telling him? He wouldn't understand.'

How does Mike understand this act?

He doesn't really, but he sees the death of Smiler as a commentary on the death of his daughter: he had put his daughter into that extreme situation but she wouldn't answer. Smiler was on that cusp between imprisonment and freedom and refused freedom – because he was afraid of the freedom in the gap. Later in the play Mike says he can understand his daughter and Smiler because they can understand him. They come to him as an answer. He says: 'I was in this place. It's 'ere.' He imagines not that he is back in the room where he killed his daughter, but that the whole room has come here as a ghost would. This is the physical centre of the play, where the whole meaning of it stands. Mike is in the gap, the place of contest, of collision, where humanness and corruption are created, and there his mind meets Sheila and Smiler. He puts them in the emptiness, so that they fill it and he can find some meaning – whereas the others keep talking of who did what but don't ask why it happened and so they could never understand. It is customary now for directors to manufacture effects (lights and music and sound). But an incident such as this can be staged only when it is understood. That totally changes the director's work.

Another character is directly confronted with Sheila's death: her boyfriend, Frank. The day after the crime, just before he calls the police to surrender, Mike offers him his flat as Sheila's dead body is still in it.

Frank is a very clean-cut young man who does everything for the sake of the law and the public good. Mike thinks that Frank has a secure humanness which will heal the rift in the house. So he puts him in his home, into his own position. But by doing so, by offering him a property with a dead person sitting in it, Mike is confronting Frank with the ultimate question. It is as if Sheila's dead body was asking him: 'Are you going to settle for the flat? Or are you going to ask the other question?' That is what she was asking Mike with her silence in the earlier scene.

But Frank's answer is: 'I settle for the flat. I want the flat. I've always liked it. I have a job now and it solves a lot of problems. All that is very nice: Let's not ask why you are dead.' He refuses the question and he compromises. He now has that flat and it allows him to slot into the position of the good citizen. Later on he will say that a flat is law and order, civilized good society – in the sense that if you have property you won't go out and rob your neighbour.

Later on in the play Frank becomes, logically, a policeman, but of the most violent, corrupted, manipulative and perverted kind.

Yes, because under that is an enormous violence: in accepting the flat for the wrong reasons, he created an ambiguity in himself. Frank actually spends each day killing himself. He has nothing to do with the crime, but he is constantly reminded that this is the place where the person he was supposed to be in love with, and was the meaning of his life, was killed. It is said that a murderer always comes back to the scene of his crime: Frank is stuck in the scene of somebody else's crime. It is as if Mike had killed him by giving him the flat as an answer to the question. He becomes a ghost in a policeman's uniform, with the traditional rage, violence and dysfunctions of a ghost. He can never be true to himself – in Shakespeare's sense in *Bingo* that you may not do wrong to any man. He follows through the idea of doing good to an extremity and it makes him very destructive. That is where innocence becomes revenge. To own the flat – and to avoid the question – is to be criminal.

He is revengeful especially against Mike. He harasses him when he is released and does everything to have him back in jail. With that purpose he even sets up a fake fight with the character called Olly at the woman's flat where Mike now lives so as to have Mike accused.

The first time he is in Mike's presence after the murder, in the visiting room in the prison, Frank is paralysed: he cannot talk because he is still asking him questions that he doesn't dare to face and has no answer for. He is himself a prison. In the staged fight, he is really attacking his own repressed self, he is having revenge on himself – that is what makes him so vicious. So the fight has to be as violent

IN ALL THESE GAPS THERE IS THE POSSIBILITY OF FREEDOM

and as appalling as possible. It also has to show his pathetic stupidity, like a drunk, very angry, who raves pathetically. He is also literally teaching Olly to be violent: he tells him what to smash, how to get angry, he hits him to tease him and so on. And Olly reacts and learns. This teaching and the learning of violence from this crazy policeman is much more disturbing than the destruction. There you see corruption processing.

So that is why the scene is called 'training'. What we see is that they literally and properly destroy the room, smashing the furniture. It all goes one step too far because Frank hurts Olly much more than he planned and eventually he blinds him by accident. He sees this as a blessing and celebrates it because he could now charge Mike with this real crime ...

This accident is a revelation to Frank. It is as if reality told him: 'Yes Frank, you are right: you perform the purposes of reality.' He set out to wound Olly to have Mike punished but it was a way of punishing him for the wound he himself received from Mike – and ultimately for the wound of the world. Now the world is healed by the wound for which Mike will have to pay. So Frank is at peace. His life is good to him. He is in a moment beyond choice, where the thing is, where it is done, as if reality had been done to him. It shows him his own wounds so that he can live with them and, because he can see them, become an agent of reality. He 'gently touches' the wounds on Olly's blinded face (just like Thomas putting his finger in Christ's wound in the Caravaggio picture) and he is thankful for his life. He finds it beautiful, he finds the destroyed room wonderful – because for the corrupt ruins are beautiful, like the ruins of Berlin for Hitler; he has destroyed the universe and he is at peace. Then he goes through a huge cosmic monologue; he comes to see and know things he normally wouldn't, until even beauty seems fatuous and meaningless. He fingers the dust and sings, 'Dee-dum. Dee-dum'. At that moment Frank shows the utter futility, the total fatuousness of a life which abandoned human responsibility. 'Dee-dum. Dee-dum' suggests something childlike, a nursery rhyme perhaps, like 'Humpty Dumpty sat on a wall' (which has to do with comic destruction) but it also echoes Edgar in *King Lear*: 'Fie, foh, and fum! I smell the blood of a British man' – or Mrs Rafi's 'Ha, ha'. The dust is also a symbol of mortality. That is the centre of the play. Everything has to be concentrated on that moment. So, on stage there is the brutal ugliness of the blinded Olly, sitting in the ruins of the flat, who keeps repeating, 'I can't see', contrasted with Frank's vision of beauty leading to the destitution of 'Dee-dum. Dee-dum'.

When he hears Mike coming in, Frank hides in the kitchen in order to knock him out by surprise (so that he can be discovered on the scene of the crime and convicted). But when he reappears he wears an apron over his police uniform.

The apron contrasts with the macho self-image and relates to Vera's destitution. It has to be a sartorially perfect police uniform – complete with cap. It shows his inner distortion. He can be in complete, icy control or is able to take advantage of things when they go wrong by chance, but there are other things he absolutely does not control – all this at one and the same time. And this is distorting. For instance, he is surprised when Mike comes back; he hits him more violently than would be necessary (and twice) but he has enough presence of mind to deliberately rip open his jacket pocket to simulate a fight. In the same way, after all this violence I wanted him to use, in contrast, a polite, almost formal phrase. But all he can do is 'speak at the normal speed' and say 'I'm tired', but once more, as in the visiting room scene, no sound comes out of his mouth. The sentence balances his various intentions. His words seem oddly almost aristocratic. Is he explaining? Apologizing? Why say anything at all? Probably the silence should be expressed by his whole body and might be even courteous? Anyway: the text induces exactly what you wouldn't expect. I wrote this part carefully to show that Frank doesn't know how to deal with his own problems but *as a policeman* he is supposed to solve society's problems. So if you play it as the caricature of a Hollywood bad cop (as it recently was) it becomes useless – because we know how to deal with that: we just have to go to another (supposedly good) policeman. The acting will not alter a word but playing in that way alters the situation I have written in the play. It is like the actors of the Royal Court during the last production of *Saved*: the director had all sorts of silly theories about the scene but the actors were never asked: 'What does it mean to kill a baby *by stoning it*?' That is the poverty of our present theatre.

You mean they were behaving like the gang instead of asking questions like Len or Mike?

Yes. You know, no director ever objected to the stoning; it was shocking and so on, but they could do it. But all of them object to the last scene … Because there is silence: 'and people will get bored and so you can't do that on stage'. It isn't so in performance. But *this* last scene should have made an audience angry more than the baby being killed, if they knew themselves or understood their society better. This means they can do nothing – or will do nothing – to stop the next baby being stoned.

5
TRUTH CAN BE VERY UGLY BUT THE DESIRE FOR TRUTH IS ALWAYS BEAUTIFUL

Understanding the people in their situation / *Summer*: a good soul is a false concept / *The Under Room*: Joan and the stranger / How people reach their decisions / *Red, Black and Ignorant*: the only way is by breaking the rules / The Palermo Improvisation / Why doesn't he kill the right baby? / *Great Peace*: the active complicity of the mother / The Woman in the wilderness / Opening the bundle, gaining humanness / The Woman didn't want to come / The Son's response.

In the two plays you have just talked about, Saved *and* Olly's Prison, *we saw violence coming from the refusal or the impossibility for the characters to ask questions about themselves or their situation. What questions would be needed to avoid this violence?*

My characters ask the questions the audience are asking themselves, even if they don't like them, or ask them only in a confused way. The questions a child asks are the questions that make you human: 'Why that?' This is the human sense of tragedy. We tend to try to solve these questions in terms of the world of things because this is the world we live in. And since the child has to learn to live in it and to survive, he or she is corrupted by society's answers. Of course it is important to provide answers but they can only be temporary because they belong to culture, to society, and they change with these. What remains is the question: What is it to be human? The Greek question – and the Greek answer was: 'Know thyself.' Now we cannot know ourselves without knowing the situation we are in. Think of the people in Pompeii carrying on their business and shopping and building houses and not noticing that Vesuvius was smoking. Or how does it happen that the guards in the concentration camps couldn't see what they were looking at? It is often said that these are the veils and mystification of ideology or personal psychology (fear of authority, and so on) but nevertheless, how can you make the people see what is in front of their eyes? Being aware of their situation? You cannot talk about anybody in a useful way unless you can talk about his or her situation. The situation depends not only on the relationships between the characters, but also on its social determinants. My point is to get into the situation to ask: 'How is it that you consent, or become co-operative, or part of this situation?' If I can show the situation, then I can show why the characters adopt their attitude to it. Take Xenia in my play *Summer*; she always gives presents, she is always smiling at people and at the same time – through her situation – helps others to kill them. This is what her situation does to her, regardless of who she is as a character.

Xenia is the daughter of an East European country aristocratic family which collaborated with the Nazis during the war. But she is a more liberal and humanitarian person. She supported the Resistance and even used her family's influence to save people. So you are unfair to her when you say she helps in the killing of people.

The play clearly states the Nazis used the culture she represented as a justification for their killings and this demonstrates her complicity. It may be confused and unwilling but it is still real and stubborn.

Yes, she meets a German tourist who used to be a guard in the death camp nearby and he tells her that he and his fellow soldiers could see her during their slaughter and they considered this young girl dressed in white as the symbol of what they were fighting for. But she firmly objects to this idea.

It didn't really matter to the victims of the Nazis if they understood why they killed them or not. In the play, Xenia is confronted by Marthe, a working-class woman whose parents worked for her family. She tells Xenia she lives in a house the foundations of which are all wrong and distort everything. So she can't be 'kind': it doesn't mean anything – it didn't stop the Nazis killing people. She corrupts notions such as tenderness and justice to serve her own (conscious or not) ends. Anna Massey, the actress who created the part, wanted to show that in the end, Xenia had 'a good soul' and in a way she wanted to redeem her. To be fair, the way acting is usually taught encourages that sort of interpretation – and after all it is how people commonly see their life. She thought Xenia meant well – but that was also the excuse of the commandant of Auschwitz. Hitler used to love dogs but if he gave all his money to PETA the heap of ashes in Auschwitz wouldn't have been lowered by one speck. Humanness doesn't exist in our emotion but in understanding the situation. In my plays emotions come from the meaning, so the actor doesn't have only to play the emotion but has to make the meaning clear. The play precisely makes the point that the idea of the 'good soul' is a false concept.

Marthe refuses Xenia's kindness, even her care, though she is dying of cancer, and towards the end of the play she even spits at her. She is making your point, isn't she?

Marthe judges her acts, not her intentions. Doing this is humanly dangerous, but also humanly necessary. The spit releases Xenia from her obsessions and justifies Marthe's attitude to her. Ironically Marthe's spit is closer to being a blessing than an insult, a sort of kiss, of freedom – rather as if Jesus had spat back at Judas's kiss. When the play was on in New York, the spit was used to show what a horrible, ungrateful person Martha was … This was partly due to the Cold War context that could put the blame on the Communists, but not only that. I also heard that when *Olly's Prison* was staged in Africa, sometimes people were applauding Mike for finally killing his daughter. All is changed by the situation you are in. It is your situation that gives your acts a meaning – unless you are prepared to change your situation.

Xenia's position is shared by another of your characters in a more recent play: Joan in The Under Room. *She is an average right-thinking citizen living in a future violently repressive society who finds one day an illegal immigrant who broke into her house to escape the police. She commiserates and sympathizes with him in such a way that she decides to escape with him.*

Joan has a liberal attitude. With her decent standards she won't be corrupted, or allow anybody to corrupt her. In this society, she lives in a sort of internal exile (as in Nazi Germany or Soviet Russia), in the sense that she would not overtly oppose the regime but she wants to keep her image of herself which confirms her as the good person who can perform good acts and can manage to live in decency. When she decides to escape with the alien, she is actually only disguising herself from herself. It is hardly more than if she changed her dress.

The alien doesn't trust her very much anyway. He mentions a war incident he was involved in as a child soldier: he was made to kill one of his parents and had to choose which one – but he refuses to tell Joan which one he chose, though she insists on asking him.

He won't tell her because he knows it doesn't mean anything to her. That was this moment that comes in every Greek tragedy when the protagonist says: 'What would I do?' And the chorus would then have said something like: 'This shouldn't happen here. The ground doesn't want this to happen', or 'Look at what's happening', or '*If stones could speak*'. But the alien only saw writing on the ground. What is written on the ground stands back, it looks at what is happening, as if the play itself was saying: 'Now you must understand what is written on the ground.' It could be written on the eyes of the audience. This is the language of reality, like silence made vocal. The alien knew then that *in that situation* a decision had to be made. Joan can't understand that. She doesn't ask for the meaning of it and this reveals that her question is only curiosity on her part. She has never been in such a position to face such an unavoidable decision and she doesn't try to imagine it. She would not be able to read what is written on the ground – she wouldn't even see it. She only believes she will understand because she can commiserate. Everybody can say: 'This is terrible! How can people do that? What are we having for dinner?' Joan's question is what 90 per cent of the audience would ask. That's why the alien answers her: 'Mind your own business! I don't want you to think about it in that way.'

Eventually the alien refuses to go with her and prefers to go with Jack, a pretend smuggler who is actually betraying refugees to the police. He seems to be the last person he should trust.

And ultimately he tells Jack (and not Joan) which of his parents he killed, because he thinks he would realize what is involved in the choice. In that situation, he would have understood decisions are not avoidable and said: 'Well you have to choose someone', instead of wailing: 'Horror! Horror! Horror!' That's why the alien can decide to go with him and not her. He also recognizes a dualism in him and he wants to contact a certain innocence which Jack doesn't normally allow himself to use. At the end Jack says: 'I never turned to crime out of weakness. I had another reason: hope.' That is the most important line of the play. The actor should always remember in everything he does that eventually he will say that line.

At the end Joan physically attacks the alien and she kills him.

She becomes completely crazy. She sacrificed everything and this man is actually saying he is not interested! It isn't only that she is rejected, but he somehow changes for her into an actual monster. It turns her world upside down completely. She contains in fact a lot of unexpressed aggression, probably based on fear. At the beginning of the play, when she discovered the alien, she feared he could put her into trouble with the police. So she acted like the police herself and began by asking *him* a lot questions. But the longer he stayed the more questions she had to ask herself about *herself* and what she is doing. These questions are too much for her to ask, she cannot face them. Joan has found the alien in herself, which is very destructive if it gets frustrated.

You chose to represent the alien with an unusual and artificial device: you literally split a character in two between a motionless 'Dummy' sat in a chair, which the other characters address, and a 'Dummy Actor' who stands still upstage most of the play and speaks his lines.

This is so that the other characters won't be able to make contact with him and this is intended to convey to the audience the idea of foreignness or otherness. The Dummy in the chair is an image of humanness with its own central dynamic. The device is artificial so that the audience can enter the territory of whys. When they looked at the Dummy, they would have asked one lot of questions: 'What is an alien?', 'How much is he like the actor?', 'How can we put the two together?', and so on.

How do you mean the 'Dummy Actor' to act?

The actor has to be like the Dummy: impassive. He gestures only rarely and usually speaks without emotion. The emotion is in the Dummy. Normally he is logical, pragmatic and coldblooded – because he is in a situation where he thinks only of how to survive. Even when he tells Joan about his most traumatic experiences he isn't demonstrating that he is a poor wounded human being. Only later, when he is asleep and relives his experiences of terror in his dream, do all his emotions, fears, indignations, all he represses, come out in this language that the others can't understand. It is like verbal bleeding.

Joan's attitude resembles actually the usual drawback of the political theatre which signs its failure. It can be relevantly analytical and critical and often sincere, but since it still tries to be convincing it tends to be compassionate or hectoring, or to hang on to strictly moral statements.

My play is actually written against all these normal left-wing propaganda plays, those awful vulgarized Brechtian tracks, where someone comes on stage to tell you what is politically obvious or say: 'How terrible!' I hate this way of telling the audience what to think. Here, I make it a job for the audience to put all these things together so that they can understand the alien *as* his situation. Of course his situation is terrible, but I want to show it in such a way that the audience can understand *why* it is terrible. I could present any atrocity as terrible, but those who commit them tell themselves they are doing good – though in their mind something must be telling them: 'It is terrible!' My play doesn't say: 'Please try to look at this in another way and be a human being.' But: 'Something in your mind will understand what I'm saying.' So I think when people angrily leave a performance of one of my plays, it is precisely because they are understanding it – but refuse to face it. In that respect, you don't need to 'alienate' things, as Brecht claimed you should – 'Do this and then notice how strange it is.' If you look at things closely and accurately enough, they are strange *in themselves* – just as discontinuities already exist in reality and can be made clear as they are. Everything is there! Brecht tried to perform some surgical operation on reality in order to prove certain things. He thought he was solving the problem, but actually he was running away from it. Drama has to penetrate the abstract relationships that motivate every action. Brecht considered you have to draw away so you can see the abstraction but I think, on the contrary, you have to enter into the relationships and demonstrate what is holding them together. It is not enough to say the relationship is absurd or mad. You have to understand why it is so. I want to see objectively inside the characters in order to see how they are attached to their social relationships. Brecht says: 'These people are blind, so turn their eyes inside out in their sockets.' No: you have to show them what they have always seen.

That means, for an actor too, to consider his character not on a psychological ground, but on a political level; that is, not as a fixed and given state, but as he is in a network of tensions and events – as you said, in his situation.

Actors and directors tend to ask themselves: 'Who is my character?' and not 'Where is the play at now?' But the most important thing about a character is that he is in the play and one has to be conscious of what the play is doing. I always begin with the situation. I define it so that there is no escape from bringing the play, and the characters, and the audience, to the moment of decision. *Then*, I show how the characters see their situation – not how *I* the author am seeing it, from a god's eye point of view, but from the point of view of human logic. My characters are there to enact various possibilities a situation offers to human beings when they are confronted by it and get involved with it. It is as if I divided one character into various roles according to the various possibilities, the particular reactions and relationships to an experience: there are all sorts of alternatives within the situation. Ultimately I am interested in how people reach their decisions because they are often totally contrary to the logic of the situation. How could that come about? I often asked myself that question: the politic argument of Marx is absolutely clear, so why is it that it is so difficult to put it into effect? This is really what my plays are about – they are not a substitute for politics.

What kind of decision according to their situation do your characters have to make, then?

They have to change their situation. This is what a play *Red, Black and Ignorant* for instance clearly states. The play articulates the threat of nuclear war (which was, as I already told you, the pervasive issue when I wrote it) with practical problems in people's day-to-day lives – but more basically it looks at the difficulty of solving problems in the sense I have just explained to you. It shows the constant repression of the need for justice that makes the whole society violent and leads not only to crimes, as in *Saved*, but also to war.

How is this practically shown in the play?

There is this Monster, we have already mentioned, who died in the forthcoming nuclear war, and who leads the play as a chorus by showing incidents or pictures out of the life that he never lived, as if it were Stations of the Cross, so that you could see the seeds of later disasters – but he is often wrong. Actually he is looking at the life the audience will have to live. It is like a detective story, where we try to explain what happened that led to a murder. At the basis of every scene of the play, there is a conflict between the practicality and the interpretation of life: the contrast between things and the control of things, between human values and the purpose of things. These contradictions could not be changed inside the situation – the situation itself must be changed. It is said that if we are nice and kind to each other we solve our problems, don't we? No, because we don't have the mechanism to solve our problems: they all are compromised in an unjust society. That is Xenia's problem. So, the only way to begin to solve the problems is by breaking the rules – and it is the same for the characters in *Red, Black and Ignorant*.

In an early scene the Monster is at school. A minor incident occurs (a Boy accidentally spat at him) which is pacifically solved by the kids,

TRUTH CAN BE VERY UGLY

but a Headmaster intervenes and, by recalling the rules, provokes a fight between the two friends.

Kids are always being told: 'Don't make a mess, clean this up', and so on. The Monster and the Boy fight out of fear – fear of the teacher, fear of the school, fear of each other, fear of their own uncertainty about themselves. This fear has been induced by the teacher because he cannot control this slight quarrel. His authority comes only from the sarcastic language he is able to produce, pretending to be full of thought, but which only disguises stupid and crude things. He seems to call the kids to order but in fact he only teaches them revenge – and this will lead to more revenge, as it does with the mafia. The scene is based on an incident in my childhood I remember very clearly; it was an accident, but suddenly the boy who was spat on became the outcast. The horror was how to get rid of the spit (the kids wouldn't have a handkerchief) and they eventually decided to tear a page out of an exercise book – which you were forbidden to do – to wipe away the spit. The same happens in the scene: they break the rules by misusing the exercise book.

In a following scene, 'Eating', we attend to a domestic row between the Monster and his wife about a book, which ends very violently.

He accuses her of hiding his book so he can't read and she accuses him of spending money on books when she has to work to buy food. The Monster becomes violent because he doesn't understand why he is being denied his access to knowledge, to thought. His wife is very practical and she thinks this knowledge is useless. But if you don't think, you don't eat, and vice versa. They fight because they can't solve this problem. This scene also is rooted in my childhood. I remember the first time I bought a book: it cost six pence and my family would have certainly disagreed that I had spent money on a book instead of food! I kept the book secret. I didn't get hungry but I felt guilty – and I enjoyed the book.

In another scene, 'Selling', we see a 'Buyer' sent by society to parents to buy their child. They stubbornly haggle about it – until they sell it for next to nothing.

'Selling' means entering the baby into the conventional society. It is a sort of bargain which consists of getting material advantage for the corruption of the child – and obviously the parents want to obtain the maximum. The transaction is self-supporting. It is contrasted with the innocence of the baby: only it knows it is wrong. As long as they don't break the rules, if they keep compromising as they do, the parents are selling themselves to society. We can also see how the Buyer negotiates through his language between the world of things and the world of values and distorts it in order to control the situation. It really is the language of the mob made aristocratic, glamorized into rhetoric. When eventually the baby is brought in, it is a theatrical prop made of newspaper, of printed language, as if it became itself this language of revenge, distortion and anger – it is the language of the popular media and the 'posh' media doesn't have an alternative to this, it only distorts it further.

We can see the Monster straightforwardly breaking the rules in the scene 'Work': he refuses to support his son if it is at the cost of a neighbour suffering.

He seems to have miraculously solved the problem, but it's not a solution at all. His son points out it is simplistic, but it is the son who will eventually discover that the only way to humanize this situation is to break the rules. By then he would have become a soldier and experienced facing an inhuman order.

This is what this incident you called the 'Palermo Improvisation' is about. We should talk about it now because I think nothing could exemplify better what you are saying. It is an exercise you directed with a group of students of drama in Sicily. You asked them to improvise on a war atrocity in which a soldier is ordered to kill a baby and is confronted with the option of murdering a neighbour's baby or his own sibling. You say all the students refused to kill the other baby and killed their sibling instead. This became the basis of your trilogy of The War Plays *(*Red, Black and Ignorant *being the first of them) as well as of your subsequent theoretical thought. There is no point in discussing its theoretical ground here, since you have already described and commented on this a great deal (especially in your* Commentary on the War Plays*) but tell me: from a practical point of view, what made the situation the students were put in during the improvisation so challenging and revealing?*

The students were in a situation where they had to decide for themselves. They couldn't say: 'I wouldn't do that but this is what my society (or my officer, or my priest) requires me to do' – or toss a coin. They had to make a choice between two innocents. Any explanation to justify a choice would have been meaningless because the two infants are equally totally innocent. So this confronted the students with their own innocence. By 'innocence' I don't mean something untouched by the world and individual experience – but a radical human knowledge. It is not abstract, it imbricates action – like the Platonic connexion between knowledge and action. The students were committed to being themselves: 'You are this person who decides this.'

You use this incident twice in The War Plays, *first in* Red, Black and Ignorant, *then once more in the third play,* Great Peace. *What actually happens to the soldier then?*

When it is enacted in *Great Peace* the soldier would have done his duty and killed the neighbour's baby, except that he finds his mother at home with two babies – she baby-sits the neighbour's child. This small thing dislodges the situation, like a pebble dislodging a landslide. The soldier then has to cope with the logic of the situation. The only explanation he gives is that he couldn't find a place to kill, which is obviously a lie – because this is like saying he couldn't find anywhere to kill in a slaughterhouse or a concentration camp – but his expression exactly explains what he feels: how anywhere in the world could be a just place to kill?

In Red, Black and Ignorant, *the baby is replaced by an old disabled neighbour. In the scene we see the soldier refuse to kill, but he doesn't say why – he only alludes to the pathetic weakness of the victim. Is there a particular incident in the scene that makes the soldier withdraw? For instance, as he talks with the old man's wife he notices that the old man is wearing a tie.*

The neighbour might have had a stroke and be incapable of talking or doing much. He wears a tie because, as often with invalids, he is washed and dressed and made respectable every morning. The tie refers to some earlier time where civility and good manners were still a workable façade – and this means he is still in this past age when people were not given these orders and has not adapted to the present times. It was also said earlier on that when his wife sends him on errands he wears a carrier around his neck so that he won't lose the bag or its contents (in the neighbourhood where I grew up I could see a mentally retarded adult set up like this by his mother). I understand one actor might think the tie made him change his mind and for another it would be the carrier around his neck, but the important thing is that it happens during this process: the soldier realizes the extreme vulnerability of the old man which makes him like a child, and he becomes aware of his own vulnerability and remembers his own childhood. This gives the soldier a formal empathy with him. As the conversation goes he begins to talk to his invisible self, revealing that he is struggling with other levels of consciousness. He goes deeper into his own mind and discovers imperatives in it. His physical surroundings seem to him to change: he remembers the weakness of being a child, but he also feels like a giant, as if he grew bigger for being faced with bigger questions – the questions of Atlas who held up the world.

The soldier in the two plays (and the students in Palermo) is not only ordered to kill by the official authority of the army: you also involve his mother.

I would never tell people how horrible war is and how much suffering it causes, and so on ... They know that and, most of the time, they think this is unavoidable, even when they are victims of it. We tend to think they are brought in by bad military leaders and financial statesmen to otherwise peacefully living ordinary citizens. The point to make is not that we shouldn't accept this (because theoretically we don't) but *why we do*. To do so, I have to show that the lives of people are ordered by ideology, even during peacetime, and *this* distorts human values and leads to war. In the plays, the officer gave the order on the authority of things, whereas the mother does it on 'the authority of human value': she tells the soldier to go and kill the neighbour's baby and not hers – or at least she states it as obvious because of the natural family links. So by refusing to commit the murder expected by his society, the soldier redefines human values because he doesn't follow what usually define these – parenthood or genes or whatever. If he did, he would have refused to be human and withdrawn from the problem – this is what enables you to perform inhuman acts. In that situation, he can be human only by defining humanness.

This responsibility of the mother is very strong in Red, Black and Ignorant: *we see her dressing the soldier, giving him the gun and sending him to the neighbour's to kill as she tells him all the good reasons to do so – and to the father, who objects vehemently.*

She is in a situation that doesn't allow her to be human, that doesn't consent to her humanity – it only makes her responsibility contradictory. But she is conscious of that when she talks about walking into her own time 'as groping blindfold inside a strange box'. She says: 'We lay the table', which is a civilized act, 'and we eat off the floor', which isn't – and then: 'What can we do in the end? Fight for our own.' She clings to what she has, and that is what everybody does. She is perfectly aware of the vulnerability of the old man and believes that he could be dead by tomorrow anyway. She says this would solve a lot of problems, but she actually forces herself to say that. Everything is contained in this enigmatic gesture: she argues, but she kisses the back of her husband's wrist 'with formal intimacy'. It is the opposite of shooting somebody – is that like killing the wrong person? By performing this formal human act she says she does understand her husband's reasons. This human act is what she really wants to do. It shows she accepts the inhuman situation but this has a cost to her, she will have to live with that.

You dramatize the Palermo situation at greater length in the first part of Great Peace, *and there again you focus very much on the mother.*

Red, Black and Ignorant is kept short so the mother understands the situation very quickly, whereas in *Great Peace,* when she is presented with the problem, she makes all the normal, conventional responses – which would be the audience's responses if they were put in that situation. She looks after her own family and has a very conventional working-class person's attitude towards authority: she is a friendly and welcoming person when everything is all right – but the killing order puts her under pressure because it involves children and then she completely changes her attitude towards her son: she shouts at him and says: 'How dare he come and say disgraceful things like that!' – but killing people is what the army does. It makes him very angry because she is pointing at what he is doing and normally just wants to forget about it – with the casual excuses: 'I'm not really doing it' or 'They're not really human' and so on. But it also enables him to comment on her hypocrisy – that the public employs soldiers to perform a job and they object that the job is being performed. This is the situation of the audience: they obviously wish the soldier would drop his gun and refuse to kill the child at the last moment – but in a nuclear-armed society, they would politically wish the soldier to be able to launch the missiles to kill his enemy's child since it is the only way the war can be won.

The mother is openly on the side of the order and supports the army. She even profits from it because her son gives her tins he stole during his round-ups of opponents.

This is the same kind of hypocrisy. I based that on German soldiers in the Second World War: they would bring home perfume or anything from Russia or France and it was much appreciated by the families who were never required to ask themselves how they obtained it.

Then she gradually accepts the necessity of the murder of her neighbour's baby and when the son fails to kill it, she sets herself up to do it with her own hands. It is only by chance that she can't.

Had she got hold of the baby would she have killed it? Or would she have changed her mind? The play doesn't have to decide. But it also doesn't pretend that she could have saved both babies, by hiding them or whatever – which could have been a prudential response but only in a human situation. Anyway, she experienced the infanticide in herself as a subjective engagement, even though it failed. This drives her mad because she experiences corruption and its ultimate emptiness. All the niceness for her son, all her initial defence of the children are torn away. The death of her own baby (when it is eventually killed by her son, to repeat the Palermo Improvisation) is secondary in that respect: it only completes her knowledge of her act. She imagines that this is

TRUTH CAN BE VERY UGLY

a punishment for it and its memory haunts the rest of the play so that the descriptions of the bombing and of the ruined world also apply to this woman's self-assault on her own mind and her inner devastation. Although she would afterwards walk over the wilderness for years and years, she cannot walk out of that room she entered to murder a baby, ever.

This 'wilderness' is what is left of the world twenty years after an ultimate nuclear war has destroyed almost everybody. The paradox is still present because we see the Woman wandering alone, carrying a bundle made of rags she treats as her baby.

She invented the baby bundle as an act of human protection, something she could hold on to. In her imagination she pretends that her baby was not dead so that she could remain in the time of security before the soldier came to kill, and carry out the function of the good mother who takes care of it. It is a dead rag but this bundle wraps up the whole human response. For her it is life itself: her psychological need for sanity, a symbolic need for understanding without which nothing survives, a pristine moral sense that judges her guilty. Keeping the baby alive is ultimately a way of keeping alive her tragic sense, which is what makes people human. As a dramatic irony, she sacrifices everything in order that her dead baby should live. That is how she deals with the paradox.

Actually we see her, rather than leaving the illusion of her bundle, abandoning to a certain death alone in the wilderness a real, living, newborn child, whose mother died while giving birth. She has this long speech to it during which she, unconsciously, unwraps the bundle into a sheet she drapes herself in.

You wrap babies in shawls or clothes, but here the Woman drapes *herself with* the baby so that she is literally inside the bundle and meets the human problematic – which is the Palermo paradox: how do you define yourself as a human being? She is mad but she recites a vision of wisdom and knowledge, through a description of human life, in order to explore the nature of life in general – not her personal guilt. It is as if sanity hidden in her, which judges her and drove her mad, is speaking through her. The cloth has a life and an authority of its own, like a hand leading her and making gestures of sanity and hope – like a sheet shrouding a statue before it is unveiled: the wind would blow it, lift it in strange shapes, sometimes it touches the stone or floats away from it and reveals it. The actress should make this unwinding very beautiful by the way she handles the sheet and drapes herself in it, like a Greek statue. Its movements should show the great wisdom inside this mad woman, that she will seek to understand what she has done, the great beauty within this ugliness, the human purpose that she carries within herself. This dirty rag, which is dead and ugly, is turned into something very beautiful – because truth can be very ugly but the desire for truth is always beautiful.

She also meets a group of ex-soldiers, her son's comrades, who all carried out their order without asking themselves questions in the way that the son did. Their position is symmetrical to the Woman's: just as she clings to the illusion that her dead baby lives, they are absolutely convinced that they are dead.

They aren't of course but this is their great solution to protect their lives. It wouldn't be so much a conscious decision, by the way, it would just soak into them: they would be surrounded by so much destruction and so many dead people that they would think: 'How can we be alive in this dead world?' Stating they have been killed, after all the people they killed themselves, allows them to abscond out of the human dilemma and solve the Palermo problem ('Who shall we kill?') for themselves.

And the Woman wouldn't admit this idea because she wants her bundle to be alive. So they attack her and tear her bundle apart to show her it is not a living child – and they will end by killing themselves to prove they are dead.

They have to do this because if now they give way on this and begin to discuss whether they are alive or not, they would be presented with the complications of the paradox – and no one among them would be able to deal with that. So it is terribly important for them to prove that nothing is alive, and that this thing that she insists is alive is just a sheet. The Woman experiences this moment as the re-enactment of the murder of her child, but she is convinced that whatever they do to it, they cannot kill it.

But at the end of the play she would unfold her bundle herself and admit it is just a rag, 'an empty nothing'.

You have to consider her journey in the wilderness above all as an exploration into the interior of the Palermo problem to find sanity again. She is lost but she has in herself the imperative to find herself. She needs to understand herself and her own motives, what happened to her, what she has done, and to work out what she would do now with it. Whatever happens to her is integrated into her problem and helps her to move towards sanity. This is also true of some of the people she meets; she even believes they are the people who took part in the events that drove her mad.

For instance, she meets a sick woman with her daughter and believes she is her neighbour and her baby who survived and grew up. First she attacks her, but then she decides to take care of her.

The daughter helping the Mother shows how good human relations can function. The Woman doesn't need this fantasy of the bundle any more to protect her humanness because she now has another human being she can 'act out the problem' on. So she uses her bundle as a genuine gift and makes it a pillow for a woman in need and she expresses humanness in a sane way and not in an insane act as when she abandoned the real baby. Later she meets a man she believes is her son, and with him she can re-live her experience and re-examine the problem. Out of that whole process, she can literally open the baby-bundle and show it is a rag and nothing more, as if the problem had been taken away by human care and human contrivances. We all can become more human, solve the problem, walk out of it.

Nevertheless, the Woman refuses firmly to join a new settlement where she could find a secure shelter in a friendly community and peacefully end her wandering. She prefers to die on her own (without the comfort of the bundle) out in the wilderness.

I wanted to pursue the problem to its limit so that it is totally defined and cannot be evaded. As a matter of fact, when I wrote *Great Peace*, I intended the community to go and fetch the Woman. But I couldn't write it. When I tried there was nothing there. It hardly ever happens to me because I usually prepare very carefully so when I sit down to write it might not be what I prepared for, but at least I can face the emptiness. This time there was just nothing. I spent several months writing this play and I couldn't end it with the Woman coming in from the wilderness: 'Good to see you! Is the kettle on?' She must have had something else to say. Then came the moment when I had written the whole thing except the last scenes, the theatre had advertised the plays and cast them and so on, and they were asking for the script for the next day – so I had to do it in the night. I finally asked her: 'Tell me what do you want and I'll write it down' and I just listened to her – and she doesn't join the new community. I was trying to invent the problem but the character was saying by that time: 'Don't lie to me.'

How would you explain her choice then?

Her role in this situation is to be implacable in insisting that they never recreate the situation of Palermo. She suffered enough to learn what it means to be human, and she doesn't need any comfort or reassurance. The most important thing she can do is to remind them that they must built a new city, a new country, draw a new map in which human beings would not be forced to perform inhuman acts in order to be human. She says: 'Make it human, and let no child lie in its cradle in a world which is not human.' This means that the new people have to understand themselves, the meaning and nature of their actions, and accept responsibility for them as a necessary part of the understanding, and are no more authority's victims. It is what she is standing for then, her demand on the survivors which she would have learned from her wanderings in the wilderness. It is her gift to the new community. She stays outside as a warning that they must face the paradox – that is, not to create the good self but the good society, or it will end in violence. She becomes its monitory foundation. And she is not at all conciliatory to them. She could have said: 'I understand your problem. Go home and have a conversation about that.' She doesn't: she rails at them, she almost abuses them! She says: 'I have seen the world drip

TRUTH CAN BE VERY UGLY

off the end of a spade, what do you understand? What do *you* know? You want me to go to the settlement only because that will be nice and comforting for you.' That is what social life should be about. If you fell down the stairs in the subway and broke your shoulder blade, you would expect me to come and pick you up, not to stand there and say: 'Build better steps!' You can't do that in real life, but in drama you do. That is what drama is about. That is what the Woman does.

The play also shows the effects of the paradox on one last character: the son. He doesn't go mad or lament; the effect on him is actually liberating.

The point of the paradox is not that the soldier realizes the monstrosity of what he did and regrets it – because he could repeat the same act and regret it again, and so on until he is himself killed. The point is that his consciousness is changed so that he would not murder again and convert what would have been his regrets into a different action and he can know his situation and act to change it.

In Red, Black and Ignorant *he says he will desert and join a group of opposition outcasts living outside the army law, and in* Great Peace *he goes back to his barracks but refuses to obey any more orders. He is eventually shot after he obstinately refused to pick up an empty cigarette packet when he was ordered to by his officer.*

This is one of the strangest scenes I have written. When you watch it, you don't believe it. It puts the nature of order under a microscope and shows its fatuousness – nothing could be more fatuous than an order to pick up a cigarette packet. There cannot be any human meaning in it. This is what he refuses. He has carried out the order. He has also been true to the paradox: he killed the wrong baby. But that doesn't solve the problem – the problem is why kill *any* baby? As a human being he can now point out the nature of the system of order and its divorce from human value. He resolutely refuses to obey an order, even if it is trivial. He shows his freedom and chooses not to pick up the packet. This is the way he gains his autonomy and protects his humanness. The Palermo paradox concentrated on a very specific incident but opened up the universal situation. That is why the solution is counter-intuitive. Throughout the three *War Plays,* the characters have to make choices that are designed to open up, to examine, that gap in which the Palermo students made this wrong-right decision. It begins with the soldier killing his father and not the weak neighbour and it ends with the Woman refusing to be rescued against everybody's expectations. The soldiers who shoot themselves to prove they are alive make also a wrong decision: they die to live. They think that is their freedom. When I came to write the last episode and couldn't, even *I* was put in the Palermo paradox by the very character I had created. It is universal. Only in the new settlement there is no paradox. They try to make socially correct decisions on prudential laws. The situation is then opened up on a social level; they don't ask themselves: 'Who do we kill in order to survive?' but 'How do we organize our lives?' But it is a hope rather than a realization: from the Woman's point of view, there is no evidence that they understood that question. She keeps insisting that human beings can never be reduced to things.

6
OBJECTS ARE PEOPLE

Objects often have strange powers / The two armchairs in *In the Company of Men* / The object in the wrong place: a glass of whisky on the floor / The meaning comes from the use / The places reflect the characters / A site is there to open a situation / The site of *The Crime of the 21st Century* like a human body / The 'grey room' / Details that can unlock the universe / Clothes are tokens of humanness / You have to play the map and the details / My directions are passports to freedom.

This empty cigarette packet the Son refuses to pick up in Great Peace *is not just any object. Earlier on in the play, when he still planned to kill the baby, he tried to send his mother away, asking her, as an excuse, precisely to buy him a packet.*

And now instead of using the cigarette packet to make it possible to carry out the order, he uses it as a ground *not* to carry out the order. The object is flipped over so that it becomes the reverse. The packet is also empty and it shows the gap where the questions of humanness have to be decided – as for the students in Palermo. For the officer the empty packet is just a piece of litter, but, since he is not obeyed, he comes to pin the whole of the world of order and authority and war on that packet – he literally says so: 'War makes this little packet very big.' It is like Mike with his daughter's cup of tea. But the Son has pinned the whole of humanity on it and he can say: 'This gap is mine and I enter it. I make my decision: I won't pick up this packet.' That is the gap of humanness. An object allows that to be experienced. That is enactment as opposed to symbolism.

Objects in your plays notably have a specific presence and activity. On stage they seem to radiate and impose some autonomous strength on the characters as well as on the audience.

Objects are obvious tools of drama. They can show what finally counts. Objects are people. Really: they talk, they act, they have their own character. You can make a king have a conversation with his throne – or someone sentenced to death with the electric chair. It won't be the same. They may be commodities but they have social and cultural values and a personal identity – and it can be the other way round: a relic might have come from a dustbin, and a crown is always made by working hands. They often have strange powers – they electrify those who use them. Sometimes they can also produce a great stillness.

Then, in what sense do you say objects are not symbolic, like this cigarette packet in Great Peace*?*

In the sense that objects in my plays wouldn't stand for anything other than themselves. If they did, they would tend to be static, or idealized, and they couldn't have any active life. A chair, for instance, is not a symbol of anything. It is just a sign of human habitation. As it is, it defines your place, so it can represent your function in society and so it may be used to show the processes of society. Objects get their meaning by the social situation they are involved in. They become *cathected* by this social meaning. But a chair is also something you can sit in, be comfortable in, eat in, ask questions in, and so on. So in a play it must always be a chair and if you do something to it, it must behave like a chair – it can break or knock your shin or whatever. The objects have to perform this dual function and follow the logic of the situation they are in. In my play *In the Company of Men*, for instance, I use chairs to show power. It is mostly set in the house of Oldfield, the major businessman, the 'king' as it were, who lives with his son Leonard whose problem is how to succeed him. There are two armchairs which are like two thrones really and which are very dramatically potent: they settle a power situation. The person who sits in it has the power at that moment. It is not only a symbol of authority because it is integrated in the practical activities of life. At the end, Leonard won't sit on an armchair but he stands on a very ordinary chair in order to hang himself and this will be an act of authority because he uses his suicide as a way of defeating his enemy, Hammond, and forbidding him to take power. When Hammond then tries to take this chair, Leonard, though hanging and on the edge of death, shoots at him with a pistol so that he jumps off the chair and scatters it and will never manage to sit on it.

Yes, but this remains a symbolic activity in the sense that the meaning of the objects remains static, since it is defined by a previously set social context.

The point is that if the situation changes, the objects begin to work differently. Then they can be used as guide through the situations. If you enter a restaurant and the chairs are on the tables, they say: 'We don't serve yet, we are sweeping the floor' – and they tell you something about work. When they are on the floor, as they should be, they say: 'Yes we have meals to serve, it's very comfortable, sit down and enjoy yourself.' The chairs tell you what the situation is. A door, for instance, is a way of getting in and out of a room, of keeping noise and the weather out – or of letting them in. But there may be occasions when the door becomes a raft in a shipwreck or you might burn it to stop from freezing. You may consider a telephone in an abstract way – but you don't when you have to use it to call an ambulance or to announce a birth. This is why in my plays I often put the object in the wrong place so that it no longer does its proper work, and can serve a different purpose. It is then *behaving* in a different way. To take another example in *In the Company of Men*: in the opening scene there is this glass of whisky left on the floor that becomes problematic.

Yes, it is very strange: this is a classical expository scene, but quite complicated, which tells us the basis of the play's financial plot, with its huge implications, but it repeatedly drifts to this glass of whisky that the servant, Bartley, had (probably incompetently) prepared for his boss.

On the one hand the play makes the distinction between the world of things, the world of business, directed by Oldfield and run by Dodds, his right-hand man, and his accountants and the world of people, and on the other hand the world of selves who create values in it. In the scene, Oldfield comes back home from a business meeting having won his great victory – it was a takeover bid, but these are today's battles. This is a fact which belongs to the world of things. Dodds congratulates him for his victory, but Leonard doesn't: he asks about his future, as Oldfield's son and heir. He wants to enter the board of the company. An inheritance is not a legal matter, it is a personal matter. It is not a negotiation of things. This implies a relationship that cannot be dealt with by accountants: it involves personal feelings – value. Even more in that case since Leonard was an adopted child, and the relationship can't stand on normal natural grounds; Oldfield has to engage himself with him more than he would with a normal son. He had to choose Leonard, and he keeps repeating this act of adoption, as if he was always testing if he made the right decision and still knows the reason why he did it – this is a matter of value. In addition to this, Dodds had just suggested to Leonard that he deceive his father by starting his own business career – as if, to become a business warrior like Oldfield and deserve to inherit his business, he had to prove that he is bad enough. This is a capitalistic reversal of values and it would mean turning the human father–son relationship into a means inside the world of things. Dodds is Eichmann, really: 'the banality of evil'. He is not even the signature put down on the form, he is the *dots* on which you put the signature. In a speech he says he is 'the power of the tool', which is the same as the power of God.

What about this glass, then?

So: the situation is set on this very fraught relationship. As Oldfield arrived Leonard served him his glass of whisky. Oldfield says it is perfect – but he refuses to drink it. There is something wrong with it but he won't admit it though Leonard insists on asking him what and proposes to sort it out for him – and really Oldfield should say: 'Oh would you mind? It has been such a hard day, thank you very much.' The glass could be the means of reconciliation, be a bridge, could close a wound – or open it. There is something in his victory that Oldfield cannot be satisfied with and doesn't control, and it is as if he found this way to bring this dissatisfaction to the surface so that he can experience it. He uses the glass of whisky to avoid Leonard's questions. The whisky cannot be dealt with just as a thing. It is something you give value to – you decide whether it is good with or without soda. Leonard and Oldfield will have to sort out something that deals with another reality and the glass of whisky opens up this other subject. From this world, Leonard will investigate himself and reality to find a meaning to both and that will be the journey of the play. Another example of an object in the wrong place is in my recent play *A Window*. The play is about the present collapse of urban society. It is set in a very poor tenement in a destitute neighbourhood, but I put a chaise longue in the room, which is out of place – it might have been inherited from an aunt. It suggests a more affluent world (the Victorian world), a better class, and carries its own sense of value with it – which has no meaning any more in a house, a society, that are increasingly impoverished and are breaking down. It shows this fragmented world where people lose their relationship to a community and to an environment and become de-socialized. A hammer and a crown have different social potencies, but in drama what defines them ultimately is the situation they are set in.

This carries on from what you explained earlier on about people who needed to be understood in their situation. Nevertheless, in this case, when the object is confronted with a changed context in which it is alien, it reveals the situation by opening a contradiction in it. But the object itself actually keeps its original meaning.

What really matters is how these objects are *used* according to this situation. What does a tree mean when you hang people on it? Or a wall when people are shot against it? Or two pieces of wood when someone is nailed on it? There is no meaning beyond the meaning we give to ourselves. An object may be objectively itself, it is changed by our use of it. If I may take another example with chairs, look how a chair is used in my play called *Chair*. The main character, Alice, uses a chair as a pretext to approach a woman prisoner she saw on the street who she believes could be her mother. She brings it down from her flat and offers it to the guard to sit on – once more the object is in its wrong place and it is as if Alice had brought the inside of her flat onto the street. But the Prisoner also begins to use the chair. First she falls on the ground to hide from the soldier who beats her, and she crawls under the chair and tries to get inside it. She puts her head inside the woodwork, to protect herself with it – as in a cage, a shelter she hides in. She actually enters a prison – it even has bars. From there she can look at her daughter and she is devastated by emotion: she has been locked up and beaten and now she is being taken to be killed and then suddenly she is faced with her daughter. That is extraordinary. She becomes incredibly strong and clenches the chair – so strongly that her guard can't get the chair from her. She tries to reach Alice so she forces her head inside the chair and breaks it. And through the pieces of the broken chair she wants to kiss her – but she can't and instead she bites her, as if she was grabbing her daughter with her teeth. It is a gigantic love and desire to touch her daughter, but it can only find expression in this grabbing and biting. So the chair, here, shows the terror the Prisoner lives in, and the passionate love that human beings can have. This domestic chair becomes part of society's structure of violence – it reveals its social dynamic.

At the end of the play, Alice will use another chair from her home to hang herself.

The chair becomes a scaffold for Alice to climb on to hang herself. This is another use. Later Billy, her adopted son, sits on this chair while the dead Alice is hanging above it. He makes it the place of his human need for her in a dead society – it becomes his mother's lap. There, the object is not a static symbol any more; it takes a life and vitality of its own and wanders around the play, as if he were saying: 'No! I don't want to be here. Move me somewhere else so I can be more useful to the play.' This allows me to use objects to show changes within permanence, to show processes. Objects combined with their use should take away all abstraction in order that everything becomes immanent to the acting. When an action in a scene comes from a relationship to objects, the motivations of the play are made concrete.

I see. But then the object is just an empty tool. How does it concretely change its meaning?

Because the use the characters make of an object throughout a play cathect it with meaning and the object carries on this meaning from one scene to another. This is what the Soldier did in *Great Peace*: he reversed the meaning of the cigarette packet by using it in the opposite

OBJECTS ARE PEOPLE 117

way. In *In the Company of Men*, after this scene with the glass of whisky, this idea of drinking will be pursued throughout the play.

This is true: for instance, two characters are acknowledged alcoholics and both are some sort of alternative models for Leonard – what he could have been if he had stayed on the street or if he were Oldfield's true son. One is Bartley, Oldfield's ex-butler, who comes from the street and goes back to it after he has been sacked. The other is Wilbraham, who comes from the aristocracy and has ruined his family's fortune and his father's company by drinking and gambling. They both have wasted their lives but they still try to hang on to their values and are reluctant to perform immoral acts.

Wilbraham grew up in that traditional aristocratic world that is full of self-confidence and that believes it is born to rule. He seems to be able to see the hollowness of that, but he really believes in all these codes of honour, this upright English way of relating to life. He destroys himself by drinking, but he won't destroy anybody else – that would be beneath his gentleman's standards – obviously he must fail as a capitalist. So he is deeply offended by being manipulated into deceiving Leonard. Bartley is equally offended when at the end of the play Leonard wants to hire him to help him to kill himself. He accepts because he needs the money he is offered, but he is torn between the money and what he has to do to earn it – in a way that Oldfield, who is an arms dealer and makes fortunes by giving people the means to destroy themselves, isn't. His protests have to be the voice of innocence. Once in the play we see him completely drunk and he has a vision of human suffering which opposes the cynical view of a global commercial exploitation of misery and war developed by Hammond, another dangerous businessman. It is as if Bartley was appalled by that suffering it will cause – and this has a great influence on Leonard. Bartley's shouting covers Hammond's voice and dominates the scene. He is then really literally blind drunk.

This is straightforward. But in this case, the play has designed a meaning for the object that influences the use of it by the characters – instead of the characters giving meaning to it by their actions towards it.

They don't have to wait for an action to find meaning: objects can be cathected by the character's imagination in the course of the play and develop from this. In my play *Have I None,* a policeman, Jams, has a close connexion with the table. At the beginning of the play, he talks about an old outcast woman he saw in a forbidden zone full of ruins. She was making huge efforts to drag a table inside a ruined house, to then climb on it and fix a picture on an almost falling wall. An apparently meaningless act – and you don't stand on tables, do you? What you normally do with a table is to sit round it and eat your own meal from your plate. The woman was very dirty, bleeding, soiling herself, so that Jams saw the table as a butcher's block. It eventually loses a leg so that the woman fell off. So, because of this sight, the table becomes cathected for him with a huge question and all the matters of life and death. Then, Jams also lives in an amnesiac society in which the authority has abolished the past – and this table seems to represent this old woman's home before it was ruined, so it belongs to the forbidden pre-amnesiac past. All this makes him particularly vulnerable about *his* table. When he talks about killing another character called Grit, the leg of his table at home falls off. When he has a quarrel with his wife about the furniture, he defends the table. And when the situation runs out of control, he falls over the table and says he is crucified on it. The table is a sort of crossroads where all the meanings meet. So, all the crises can turn up in that table. In that way an object combines the situation in the real world and the psychology of the one who uses this object. More generally objects are to me a means of defining characters, as soliloquies were for Shakespeare – they can be to us like Hamlet's skull. Objects are part of the psychological world: they contain the self's problems with itself and society. Objects are used in human life and our common humanness is in our relation to objects, so that a chair may contain a way of life, a cup – whole or broken – may contain the universe. An object is not static because humanness lies in its use and the actor's use of the object passes over into the watcher's use. This is a creative-materialism. This doesn't work only for props. For instance, my play for young audiences *Tune* deals with the barriers that people create between themselves and it uses the visual metaphor of the wall.

There is a boy who has shut himself in his room because he is defying his mother's new boyfriend – and they have to talk to him through the

OBJECTS ARE PEOPLE

wall. When he needs to confront the boyfriend he doesn't come out of his room, or walk through the wall, you write that he becomes *the wall.*

Yes. When the boy turns into the wall (which is interesting to stage), what was his prison he turns into his freedom, because a wall has two sides and two meanings: you can protect yourself behind it and keep people out, but it can also imprison you. So he reverses the meaning of the wall and turns his weakness into his strength. The point is that he feels as strong as the wall – as he later explains. And once the boy has declared his freedom and found his strength, he is immediately faced with the violent reaction of reality: his future stepfather attacks him with vicious violence, and his mother will reject him, and so on. It is as if he had knocked on the wall of a library and *all* the books came down and open at once – this neat order is suddenly converted into chaos, as if a new dimension has taken over. In the end the boy meets a girl who uses a blanket in the same way he used the wall: she believes it protects her from the cold but only because its red colour makes it warm. So he realizes this imaginative device that was a form of strength for him can be a weakness and a deception. That is the difficult thing: everything of value can be the opposite of itself – otherwise it cannot have any value. When they are cathected and used by the characters, these things affect the whole play and make everything react. I can use any element of the set to show the psychology of the characters in this way or to support the situation, make it not only material, but meaningful, active – for instance, the house in one of my latest play, *Innocence*.

It is a small derelict farmhouse in the mountains where an ex-soldier lives in hiding. You call him the Son.

The house represents his subjective self – the inside part of him. The house is falling to pieces, it needs repair. It is partly covered by tarpaulin – just as the Son used to hide his face behind a balaclava before he escaped. It is an insecure hiding place but it has this big view of the distance beyond. The Son only brought his problem with him to the house – he has not repaired it. He doesn't know anything about himself and tries to escape from himself. He has never knowingly met his mother since he was an adult – they met but he didn't know it was her – and when she turns up again, he begins to repair the house – and this will be a first step to finding a way of solving his problem.

The house has no door and the Son strongly refuses to have one put in.

During the play, the house is taken over by another character, who actually repairs it – and the first thing he does is put a door on it. A door marks the boundary between the outside and the inside of a space – so in this house it is the boundary, the access point between the world outside and inside the self. At one moment, the Son stands in the doorway and says he doesn't know where he has been all his life, then he tries to open the door and it crashes to the ground. It is also in the doorway that the woman who turns out to be his mother appears to him. Another example of how a set can be used in relation to the characters could be the scene on the front line in *Eleven Vests*, which we talked about earlier on.

It is when the Student-soldier meets the Enemy who leaves him this question in his foreign language after he had bayoneted him.

That's it. It happens at the gate of this strange tower isolated in a desert countryside. Before the surrender and murder and so on, we saw the Enemy on his own, isolated from the others, at the top of this tower, which is like a cellar near the sky, outside the realms of authority. It is like looking into somebody's mind. He went there not only to have a sleep but in order to be with himself. There, he talks about himself in a very direct and intimate way that nobody else in the play uses. The tower becomes the place of his memories, and he is surrounded by the death of his comrades. But the tower has its own memory of a past because there he finds an object: a toy train left by a child. The Enemy holds it as he speaks but the train speaks to him, in its own language. It says: 'Choo'. And it is the centre of the play. So we know the 'enemy-child' completely as a human being and this tower has really become a human place. The tower stands in the middle of a wild open grassland, like a prairie, with ditches but mainly flat. Earlier on, the school scene had a wall, gates, in a town, and everything was closed, comprehensive, controlled. The bayonet instruction scene was on the parade ground in the barracks: these were spaces belonging to authority. Here, the authority is far away, manipulating but distorted. Its voice has become an indistinct (for the audience) sound at the end of the soldiers' intercom – from the headquarters – and the Student can turn it off when he kills. It is as if authority had slowly withdrawn to its safe position, in its bunker, and its rules didn't apply at the tower any more.

And how does this affect the action?

What happens now is out of range of authority and the scene is between the victims of authority. *They* now have authority and responsibility. The soldiers are in a situation where they will have to improvise, to speculate, to invent, to think, and that means to question themselves: 'What am I doing? What authority do I have in that situation?' Then the Student can really do something he can assume the responsibility for, and this happens at this tower that has been cathected by humanness by the Enemy when he was in the attic, as I described earlier on. When you use its elements in that way, the stage is not a mere set any more but a *site*, a place produced by the situation as it were, a location designed to fit in with what we intend to do with them or at them. Think of act two in *The Cherry Orchard* where the characters are in the countryside; they are suddenly away from their normal surroundings, in a landscape where they hear this strange noise. I have been very conscious of the importance of designing spaces as sites from my very first play, *The Pope's Wedding*: there is the village green where the characters play cricket and the pub and these create various forms of sociality, there is the hut where a hermit is shut in like somebody locked up in himself, and it contrasts with a family situation in other scenes. The relationships between these sites are fundamentally important.

So, if I try to sum up: a site is a place that exposes the situation and materializes its determinants, so that both audiences and characters can experience them, is that it?

Talking about site means talking about the situation. We use a site as a way of opening a situation. Anything in a society that is relevant to the situation, to its development, its crisis and problems can appear in a site – and possibly as an element of resistance to its problem. It is like a net where fishermen catch not only their fish, but also things they were not looking for. Anything on the site is an actor: it interacts with the characters. They are using it and it uses them. So the site is never neutral, it is always contributory – and in reality, even the natural environment is not passive in relation to human beings. Therefore a site is not just the objective reality, because it also relates to the culture and the psychology of the characters on it. A site is dualistic in that it is subject both to the laws of nature and to human subjectivity. If the site is changed – because society changes – so are the people on it and the site then reflects their changes and becomes psychologized. Since each element in that site retains its autonomy and is a participant, the relationship between a person (or a community) and that site is abrasive. But this always has to be seen from the point of view of the individuals, not of the society. Anyway, whatever you are doing the two cannot be disentangled. If we only rely on the objective world, we let ideology give it its meaning and then we are blind: we don't know who we are, we don't know what we are doing – so we keep bumping into the site instead of building a relationship with it. And we cannot either withdraw into the purely subjective because there we would keep bumping into the objective, into society in ourselves – because we construct ourselves out of that relationship. This is what I wanted to deal with in my play *The Crime of the 21st Century*: human beings in relation to their situation, but prior to their confrontation with the immediate presence of the forces of society – this means to look at the social pressures internalized, as people carry them in their heads.

The play shows people who have escaped from a future repressive society into a dry desert of ruins out of the law's control. They are chased by soldiers we never see and they meet in what remains of a house – hardly more than collapsed walls – that a woman has turned into a habitat. How does this relate to that psychological situation you describe?

The site is mapped out to provide the basic elements of the situation that human beings are concerned with and make them human: they need care and protection (that is why the place is basically a house), they have to eat, to rest, think, imagine, plan for the future, they are connected with the outside – and the site itself dies towards the end of the play when a character decides to tear off the tap that supplies water. The site is almost like a diagram of the anatomy of the human body, where everything is placed according to its function. It is like Rembrandt's *Lesson in Anatomy*. The characters wander around themselves like Lilliputians over the gigantic body of Gulliver, being themselves and exploring themselves. It is almost as if their body were outside them, and they could turn the interior of the body into the stage in which they are living.

So this is why we never see the external world in the play – the low remains of wall hides the horizon. But the characters themselves don't remain inside the site to examine themselves, they constantly come and go outside.

This wall marks a boundary between the site and the social world outside, between the self and the material reality, the subjective and the objective – it is like the human skin. On the site, people have to define themselves and they always do this in relation to the outside world, where authority is and manipulates them.

When they go outside, it is always an experience of violence for them. One of them is caught by the soldiers, who mutilate him because another character has betrayed him to assure his own safety. And the two women had been banished from their community.

They have to find out what is the human logic behind all these things happening to them on the other side of the boundary. Therefore they need to understand how to be responsible for what they are doing on this side of the boundary, on the site. So they have to be constantly negotiating on the boundary – this is our possibility of making society more human.

At the end of the play, the site turns into another place, completely different, which presents one final picture. It becomes an empty sort of prison cell you call the 'grey room'. Is it another place? Another site? Or the site itself morphing?

Here the play desires to open the site up into a wider sense. It should come into place like a natural, inevitable, conclusion of all that happened before and enclose the whole site – not be smaller than it. The image works such as Piero della Francesca's *Dream of Constantine:* you see an open tent in a camp, strongly lit in a night scene and it looks like a picture suddenly torn open inside another picture. The tent seems almost bigger than the picture it is part of and it has an extraordinary luminosity, as if the colour itself was luminous. This is about the dream of an emperor; the tent is guarded by soldiers as if the dream was incorporated in the ideology. The picture is also strangely ambivalent because the tent has a shape that Piero will also use for the hill of Golgotha, the site of the crucifixion. But in this painting it is turned into something luminous – a piece of heaven? Ideally at the end of my play the whole stage should appear to be inside this big luminous tent. It is not to suggest that the site was a prison, but that a prison is the result coming naturally out of the site. And so it is the only possible site for freedom.

This final room is inhabited by one of the characters, Grig, who just takes a few paces, stares at a square stone strangely standing in the middle of the space, and eventually howls seven times.

The stone carries the idea of the bricks of the desert ruin in the rest of the play and elevates it to a lost ideal. It is like an empty classical pedestal. It is expected that a statue stands on it, but there is nothing. Grig stands next to it and walks a few steps, wearing a medical smock, which is near to a classical toga. He is like a human statue that can't get on its pedestal. He doesn't even try to reach the stone – he just wanders around like a monkey in a cage. His howls come from *King Lear*: over the dead body of his daughter Lear says: 'Howl, howl, howl! O you are men of stones.' Grig is Lear alone in the world maybe – but it is worse because he is alone with himself. I copied Shakespeare and wrote 'howl' though it would normally be a stage direction ('He howls') and not the sound, but it is better this way, to make the direction the sound – as if Grig was describing objectively not just his personal pain but the world's pain or humanness's pain. In this picture, there should still be the possibility of humanness. The stone and the walls, for instance, should look like natural materials made artificial by a machine and so they strangely evoke something human. It is a scene of the end of time, in a frozen eternity, but it still breathes of a human memory.

OBJECTS ARE PEOPLE

This notion of site allows you to put what would be general ideas down to a material form on the stage – and at the same time they make the stage a concrete metaphor, an image, that can be caught by the imagination. However, once the situation is so firmly set, how can you avoid abstraction so that audiences can connect with it and so that things can remain concrete and move inside it?

It is the site of the action. So movement and language are also events on the site. The site makes these things concrete, not abstract 'art'. Everything is 'site', and nothing exists in isolation – even the human imperative relates to a site – there is no god or power outside the site that controls it. To write a play, you have to know about politics, economy, sociology, history and so on: the widest possible reference to know all the structures operating in a society. You need these big patterns because they are part of human reality, the structures we are in. But you need something immediate and absolute that pins it on the individual moment, something that says: 'You are at this moment.' So the problems are not abstract – they are: *now, you*. Because when you deal with these big abstract structures you think you are talking about values, but you aren't really. Ideologies such as religions tell you the meaning of reality and also what to do in reality. But this only consists in turning values into facts – whereas value is something you can only create for yourself in experience. Now late capitalism has taken over from religion, there is no unit of value any more and nothing can have any meaning – instead everything has a price. So we have to find a way of creating some sense of value and you can't do this without some unit of measurement. Therefore values really come down to small acts or simple objects, whatever they are. The simplest objects can be caught up in the interpretation of life. So when I write, I base my descriptions on details: the significant moment in an event, the significant part of an object – and dramatize round that. It is dramatically necessary to find the point that an audience will immediately recognize and know exactly where they are. Then they can relate that to the other events in the play. The audience are reacting with their whole imaginative self and that makes them very observant. They can catch the smallest nuances. For instance, in *The Balancing Act*, Viv makes a speech about a huge ship full of people dancing which sinks when one single small grain of sand falls on it. It always makes a strong impression on kids because it deals with the scale of things. The young person's mind naturally accepts that things would normally balance themselves out, and work themselves out – but one grain of sand can completely upset the balance. This single small thing that can sink a ship provides them with a concept that changes the idea of balance. And it works just the same for adult audiences.

This is what you called earlier on being 'cathected' with meaning.

Absolutely. Generally, the plainer the object, the more power and the larger significances it delivers to be used: a cup, a chair, a coat, even a button. On stage they can enact the universe. King Lear also says (before he says 'Howl, howl, howl' before he dies): 'Undo this button.' I am fascinated by this line – and I often refer to it in my plays. It is an image of order but also of disorder. Those very simple involvements make the abstractions real, they put them into focus. Such small things are keyholes to that other human reality where the meaning of things really is, where my plays and my acting roles lead. Racine has this extraordinary power (the opposite of Shakespeare, really) to put the most immense human passions in the consistent form of verse so that they become the most radiantly simple and insistent. In the same way, you can make the world work for you in drama by the use of objects, they can unlock the universe – if I may put it in that elegant phrase. This is what the Son in *Great Peace* does with his packet of cigarettes. Can you see now how different it is to symbolism? This has to be the starting point of interpreting the situation – and of any drama. To take another more down-to-earth instance, in one of my recent Paris plays, *People*, we see a woman who can tell the lives of people she has never met from their clothes and the way they have been worn – as you can tell an animal by its spoor.

This is a very moving scene: this woman collects clothes from dead bodies in mass graves for reselling. She sits to sort out which ones she could sell and she manipulates these miserable pieces of clothing, trousers, shirts, socks, a boy's jumper, which are all that is left from the dead.

She examines each one very closely to find out any mark or tear on

OBJECTS ARE PEOPLE

it and by doing so she deduces a lot of information about the wearer so that she can describe him, his character or his social position ... She can read the clothes like a fortune-teller can read your palm and say simply by looking at a small jumper how this child had been treated by his mother. It is as if the clothes would bear a record of their past and be collectors of the places in which they were – could you imagine all the movements that have been made within those clothes while somebody wore them? But she also reads in them the situation of the whole economy and society. Most of my clothes, for instance, are made in China, but we don't live in China – what does that say of my society? Clothes also deal specifically with the social identity. They are an image society puts on the individual. It is very obvious with uniforms: you can clearly see a prisoner or a soldier is owned by their society because this is stamped on their clothes. There once used to be sartorial regulations for each class. So you put your society on with your clothes. They design a map of society. But since clothes are an interface between the personal and the social, they work also in the other way round and are badges of identity: they tell who you are, more than a name. So this woman is able to talk about a community and in a way identify the flaws that would have contributed to its collapse. You can see that to survive, she reduces clothes to a price (for selling) – but she can still identify them with their value in a human sense.

Clothes aren't just any mute objects. Their shapes more or less imitate a body, so that even before they are marked by their wearer's use, they are naturally cathected with an idea of humanity.

Clothes are tokens of humanness. Macs, for instance, are very anonymous garments but this sheer anonymity impresses their individuality. A mac is a compact item of clothing: it doesn't have legs but it falls from the shoulders to below the knees with two arms. Its shape is quite close to a human being. A coat can serve all sorts of purposes (dress coat or a uniform and so on) but a mac is just there to defend you against the weather. It can also collapse completely, unlike a coat. So if a coat is a form of clothing, a mac is a form of nakedness; it is much more like a human skin. Bartley, as I have already mentioned, says he doesn't want to die in a mac.

Bartley is a working-class character who has lost everything and really hits rock bottom. He says this as he wakes up with a hangover in the derelict house – and he is wearing a mac. It seems that here lies his ultimate, desperate, decency – he adds he wouldn't dare to show his face in the other world wearing a mac.

Yes, it is a strange haunting line – my favourite in the play. Bartley thinks if it happened it would mean he has exhausted all his chances. He would have ended up destitute, a life thrown away, wasted. Clothes are also able to reveal human presence. In *A Window*, a boy can communicate with his dead mother through her clothes – and allows them to communicate back to him. It is just a pile of clothes but he addresses them as if she was really there. He needs to demonstrate to her what he is doing – that is, defending her against his father. Imagination can do that. It directly *enacts* his relationship to her, as his own experience, which is its real meaning. These are the small things that make the generalities real. I can use this ability to cathect the audience. In *The Under Room*, which we talked about earlier, I make the Dummy Actor give his clothes to the Dummy, to cathect it with human presence. Then he sits in the Dummy's chair, and the two must be very close together so that we could feel it is the Dummy who brings the Actor to the chair and creates him – and not the Actor who simply takes the Dummy's place, as a child might a doll. This reverses the situation of the play and allows the audience to question it again because the Actor is in the same place as the audience watching the Dummy.

How can actors or directors deal with these small things and objects to make them as meaningful as they potentially are? Do they have to point at them for the audience? Or to make them bigger? To push them forward?

Not at all! They have to use them with their own potency. And it can be huge. I remember in the first production of *The Sea* (which was brilliant), during the funeral service that ends with this fight between the ladies, the actress playing Mrs Rafi, Coral Browne, showed she was getting cross with her companions just by starting to tap the side of the urn with one finger. The moment she did that the audience was so excited by what was happening, it seemed the whole theatre erupted

OBJECTS ARE PEOPLE

into laughter. Everybody was already laughing before this – someone in the row in front of me stood up pointing and said: 'Look what she's doing!' The small things in my plays are projected to the map of the world. If an actor tries to act the map, he becomes rhetorical, and if he acts the details without the map he gets lost in triviality. The details are like the stones you throw in water: they set up ripples. You can't act or direct ripples – so in my plays you have to get the details right. It is only then that you can have the big things right (as Alain Françon once told me) – the play as a whole. My plays don't say to audiences: 'Can you understand this?' They give a form of measurement by which they can understand. So I have to describe them accurately enough. For St Teresa, hell is a little door in the corner of a room, which I think is a brilliant thing to say – but as a dramatist *I* have to ask what is the number on the door. Everything I do about directing and acting a play is actually an attempt to give you *means* to understand, because you can experience things – and this is what we are always doing as human beings.

You are offering actors and directors the same opportunities to experience with your stage directions – which are notably numerous, very precise or odd and unexpected.

My indications are not prescriptive. They are meant to challenge the conventional meaning of a situation which inevitably occurs when it is left to speak for itself. They are not instructions about how to do things. Instead they are re-describing the situation. But the 'what' does not say 'how' to act, on the contrary: it demands creative freedom and insight in performing the 'how'. The directions don't say: 'Now do this, this way!' They just say: 'Open *this* door – not *that* door because it opens to another play.' The point is not to *allow* the actors freedom, but to give them the *responsibility* of freedom. My indications are not orders, on the contrary: they are like passports to freedom. The actor playing Frank in the chest in the scene of *Restoration* we talked about earlier, instead of banging his heart out, he could as well just scratch with one finger and the concentration in that would be so great it could fill the whole auditorium. Then the actor would be entering into the audience's life. It is true my plays often make enormous performance demands on actors and most directors don't understand this. An actor is not a paint brush. He has to invent a paint brush in order to do the picture. The director works with the mental and physical resources of an actor, therefore he has to clarify the situation for him. His job is to convey the problems to the actors, not to solve their problems for them. That's why rehearsals shouldn't be about 'making things work' – because this is simply glossing over the problems. They should be about finding out what things are. The job of a director is to get the actors to articulate the two dimensions together, the whole and the detail, because playwriting is always about combining the particular things and the generality.

7
THE KITCHEN TABLE AND THE EDGE OF THE UNIVERSE

I like to write opening scenes / *A Window*: how can evil be part of the daily routine? / *At The Inland Sea*: tea spilt at breakfast / Accepting the responsibility for the world / The old lady from the future / Of course we live in the material world, but why is that? / *Coffee*: the house that stands on the cliff in Babi Yar / Coffee spilt on a mass grave / The three sites on the cliff / I alter the sites: the imagination before Babi Yar / The bottom of the ditch: a struggle to become human.

Could we come back to this point you made about objects and details in your plays being units of measurement? It seems that what makes all these 'small things' close to the audience's experience is not only that they are small but that they are mundane. The real point of this scale is not so much a contrast of big and small but of the ordinary and the extraordinary, isn't it?

When you write a play you have to choose situations where something anomalous, out of the ordinary, takes place and the consequences can be extraordinary and affect everything. But it is important that everything starts from the mundane, normal world, or what is based on it. That's why I like to write opening scenes. After I have done that I feel I can stop because what will happen next is obvious. One of their functions is to show everything is very ordinary so that the audience can identify with the world – then the play can dig into that setup to look at the stresses inside normality and dramatize the reactions people have towards them, and as it goes on the world becomes stranger and stranger ... The drama has to begin immediately to involve the audience and you have done that well if they are intrigued. For instance, *The Under Room* begins with the Dummy who has broken in but it's all right, the police will sort it out. The irony is of course that from the beginning the burglar is the one who is absolutely honest, candid, because of his experiences, whereas Joan, the normal citizen, in fact isn't. She doesn't know herself. This is what the play will be about. It is the same for a play like *Tune*: it is just a worried mother who has a problem with her son, a situation that can happen in any home – though it is not all that normal for a child to lock himself in his room for three days, but it is a normal abnormality, as it were. The actors have to make the first scene very normal. You shouldn't suspect that the boy will become the wall of his room or his stepfather will slash his wrists with a piece of glass – and that the play will lead to this extreme imagery of the sacrifice of Isaac. It is the same also in *A Window*: to begin with there is only this woman, Liz, making up a bed – then her husband arrives home. A normal situation.

What goes wrong there is that Liz is upset by something that shouldn't belong to reality because it is too horrific: she read in a newspaper the account of a woman who willingly blinded her kid with a pair of scissors. It is a bit like Mike with 'the lad just leaving', she becomes obsessed by this and it affects her whole life.

She is above all frightened by the fact that the woman talked about it as if it were very normal, as if she thought it was a perfectly obvious thing to do. It is like these people in Rwanda, for instance, who started killing their neighbours from another ethnic group and later say it happened in a normal way. We come back to what I said earlier on. It is terrifying: how can evil be part of the daily routine? Of the world we are part of too? Liz would deny that the world could be destructive in that way, but in her mind she knows it is.

She brings this event into her own experience and it reveals something of her situation so overwhelming that it leads her to commit suicide.

She is obsessed by this story because later, as a mother and a drug addict, she doesn't feel able to take care of her son – and in fact we see her being very destructive towards him – and she can't face it. She has a speech in which she examines this as an act of destruction that exists in that normal world. It is like a view from the inside, *a view from the window*: she looks at the window and she sees a crime committed on the street, and the street just goes on as normal. And this frightens her.

How does this appear in her speech?

It combines a description with little actions in which she enacts each thing she talks about in relation to an object. She begins with her own relationship with her son – who is asleep in front of her – and she tears a sheet to strips, as an act of destruction – the opposite of care. Then she handles the scissors and imagines in great detail the act of blinding the child. Then she rests her head on the chair while her son is asleep and she brings the whole world into it: she speaks about war: 'You see it every day. Famine. Kids' bones wrapped up in old skin. War. Fighting. Tanks, bouncing in the dust. Clouds of it.' She articulates it with street imagery: 'The piece of bread in the street. The long streets. The piece of bread dropped in them for a filling. The city is a stone sandwich.' These are strange combinations but they are very careful metaphorical descriptions which recover language and make it speak for us. When she has finished, she goes off as if she was going outside but beyond that door she hangs herself. Before that, she puts on the most crude, stupid piece of music: this is the banal world of the city and this is the world her boy wakes into. The normality comes to cover the violence. And the boy dances to the banal music of the city – while his mother is hanging herself in the next room, and he has to tidy the room he is in, clear away the torn strips of sheet. Different layers of different experiences are put together. The play as a whole assembles fragments of existence and falls in three parts, as in Francis Bacon's triptychs – but it has a fourth panel that is the window, so that the audience itself would look through the glass at a fragmented world. The play ends with the boy looking at the audience, that is through a fragmented world in another direction, into the world outside. It reverses the view from the window to question the normal world we are in.

In your first play for young people, At The Inland Sea, *the intrusion into the average reality of another cruder reality is materially accomplished.*

We see a Boy quietly drinking his breakfast tea, when a Woman holding a baby appears like a ghost in the middle of his bedroom, coming from a gas chamber in Auschwitz.

In this play I am really observing the relationship between normality and abnormality. It seems surreal but it all comes out of a very domestic ground: the Boy has to make his bed in the morning before he goes to school and he spills his tea and his mother shouts at him. I was told that children attending the play were most shocked by the moment when the Boy spills his tea out of fright at seeing the Woman. This image strikes them more than the subsequent gas chamber scene! They cannot relate to gassing people but they can immediately relate to spilling the tea – which is like committing some sort of offence. It becomes their relationship to the killing: it matters to the kids because of the tea. Curiously enough it gives a reality to it that talking about blood on the floor would not have. It is then as if all these events happened between the tea leaving the cup and the tea hitting the floor. The play presents the audience with this extreme situation of this Woman in a gas chamber and the shaking cup of tea can bring it into a domestic dimension. The world of Auschwitz and the world of the schoolboy who spills his tea are brought together, and together they create the present time for the audience – here and now. This breaks up the usual connexions between things so that the mind can make its own connexions. It has to ask why, to seek for meaning, to search for where it is. This is what the Boy does in the play: he comes to the questions of Auschwitz not because he is being told in school to study it for the examinations, but in his bed, by having this fantasy. It is a clear example of the way drama works.

Is this because you brought the experience of Auschwitz inside their everyday experience that the young audiences can get this unit of measurement?

Yes, but not exactly. It goes a little further. The point is more that they could understand that their experiences have the potential of the extreme in them. The play deals with the tragedy of the previous generation but it is also a tragedy of the Boy's world. I regard the play as a rite of passage towards a young person coming to understand his situation, coming to be himself. The title refers to a world inside you to be explored – and so to the activity of drama itself. In this possibility of the extreme, the Boy can experience his and his mother's problems and his relationship with her and how he negotiates with that. When the play is enacted properly the young people would be situated in a way that is productive for them. It wouldn't be an intellectual puzzle. They would be given means of judging that would enable them to give value to it. It wouldn't simply be a reference about themselves – 'Have I passed my exam?', 'Does my mother understand me?' – but it would lead them to approach broader and deeper problems. Actually, I try there to reproduce the experience I had when I saw *Macbeth* as a child myself. When Macbeth reaches for the dagger, he does what you do at the meal table when you eat and reach for your knife – but Macbeth's dagger is invisible, but it works like the spilt tea.

The Boy's mother is only concerned about her work and his studies – the world of things – and this woman coming from Auschwitz presents him with another sort of problem: she begs him to tell a story that would save her baby. She brings him inside the gas chamber but he can't find a story able to stop the gassing. All he can do is first to stop time, make everything stand still.

The Boy stops time because he can't bear what he sees. It is impossible, unacceptable! He doesn't want this to happen and he stops this happening. Curiously the people in the gas chamber when the time is stopped don't want to be saved. They want to die because they are in the middle of nothing.

This is it, he won't save them; when, later on, he will restart time, the people go on dying. He has completed nothing.

That is the past and unfortunately you can't change it! You must let the past happen and be itself and the Boy has to accept reality for what it is. He has to tell himself (because he is imagining it all) that this really happened, in its completeness as a human fact. Letting the people die is more a way of accepting what is actually happening in the present. In this sense you are responsible for the past. So the point is not to deliver a happy ending, but to produce the reassurance that you can deal with this problem.

At the end of the play he can finally tell a story, but it is quite enigmatic. In what way does it answer his problem?

You need a story that would relate you to your life and structure the meaning of certain events happening to you. The whole point of a story is that it is not an interpretation of your life: you have to *live* the story. That is the difference between being told a story and an enactment in a drama. And it is what the Boy's story is about. It tells about a man who hears singing from a hut, but when he goes in it, it stops, and when he goes out it starts again. The hut is empty when you come into it but it is full when you leave it. It is only outside the situation that he can know its reality – outside the house that he can hear the music inside the house. That is a reversal of what has happened in the gas chamber. The meaning would be: you found something but you can only keep it if you go on searching for it – that is the logic of humanness.

You also introduce a ghostly character, very bizarre in that context: an old lady, dressed in an old-fashioned way, who constantly laughs at all the horrible things the Boy tells her.

I wanted to put the play in a very wide perspective because children are vulnerable. The idea of babies being killed is disturbing and they could fear they would never get out of this. So I developed this idea of a time when we would be so civilized that we could see how absurd human history is – like the Greek gods laughing from Olympus at the mortals. This Old Woman lives out of history, so she can look at it free from any objective, scientific or philosophical point of view, and find it terribly funny that people could do anything as stupid and pointless as gassing other people.

Do you really think that if someone can have enough ability to distance himself or herself from it they will find it funny?

Well, I don't really, because *I* don't find the burning of Joan of Arc or ancient human sacrifices funny. But this is actually dramatically profound because tragedy and comedy are very close intellectually and, strangely, in meaning. This is also true of children. They can say: 'Yes, how absurd!' The Old Woman opens up an extreme in the play in a way an angelic, supernatural figure couldn't. Just as it is Macbeth, the villain, who releases the problem for the audience and not those who come in the end to restore law and order. She looks an eccentric person because she is ambiguous. There is a pathos attached to her: she is carrying under her elegant smock a dress corrupted with the record of the crimes of humanity, the symptoms of human sufferings. When she tells about her dress covered with the tears of humanity, she does it with a great sense of the tragic. Then, she doesn't laugh any more. She shows the stains of blood and tears. So the play makes a strong point of identifying everything with the kitchen table that the kids would know and then it deals with a real extreme – people being mass murdered – and it can do extraordinary things: going into the past, jumping into some distant millennium in the future, or stop time. So it is really as if the edge of the universe was brought to the kitchen table.

You mean this fantastic dimension with its extraordinary events trespassing on the mundane is an exposition of the general understanding in the play?

I mean the ultimate meaning of human life and reality can only be found on the edge of the universe. The classical idea is that to find knowledge you go on a journey – to the Deep North, Damascus, or until the end of the universe, as it were. There, you discover something that gives you understanding – according to the Christian pattern it would be the City of God. But I say you might find yourself on the edge of the universe when you are stuck on the kitchen table. They are not two different places but two 'realities' and they can only come together in the gap. You remember when we were talking about *Olly's Prison*, the moment when Mike brings his dead daughter and Smiler back to him in the room itself and says, 'I was in this place. It's 'ere'? Well, that really is one of those moments when the edge of the universe is brought to the kitchen table. Then Mike faces the whole meaning of reality and he has the feeling that everything can be solved. But the edge of the universe does not produce its own illumination for you. Frank's 'Dee-dum. Dee-dum' is also pronounced on the edge of the universe: he went to the extreme of his experience but he discovers only wilderness, the ultimate desolation. What the Dummy in *The Under Room* reads on the ground is actually written on the edge of the universe – and this is why it was out of reach for Joan who can only see the kitchen table.

This articulation you suggest between the material life and its deepest, human signification completes the idea we have been exploring for some time now that the big questions can cathect small things, and can be found in everyday situations, expressed by ordinary people ...

It is not only that they *can* but that they *have to* – because we learn everything from what is out there, in the world. To be alive is to be practical: you negotiate with the site you are in. On the kitchen table you do the mechanics, the economics of existence. But all the practical situations ask the question: Why should it be so? What is the total meaning of this? That is Leibnitz's question: 'Why is there anything rather than nothing?' Because we are human beings, we say: 'Of course we live in the material world, but why is that?' In the past, the edge of the universe has always been owned by God or gods. In modern times it is owned by the market – and what is terrible about it is that it only knows the kitchen table and it pretends it is the edge of the universe. Drama deals with the kitchen table *and* the edge of the universe – this really is what it is about. And a play is here to say: 'Yes, but how do you live with the edge of the universe?' My characters have both feet on the ground, but they are always asking themselves: 'What is the meaning of reality? What does it mean that two and two make four?' A question for an actor to ask is: 'Where is the character now? Is he at the kitchen table or on the edge of the universe?' For instance, in my play *Coffee*, I show a young man, Nold, at the beginning of his experience, studying in a book open on his kitchen table, to get a job which would enable him to do constructive things in society – this means he tries to make a relationship between the world of values and the world of things. But someone comes to corrupt him and he will bring him where the truth of his situation is, the edge of the universe, and this is the cliff of Babi Yar.

Babi Yar is the infamous site in Ukraine of a horrifying massacre perpetrated by the Nazi death squads in September 1941; within two days they assassinated the entire Jewish population of Kiev (some 33,000 people) by shooting them with machine guns on a cliff over a huge ravine – they fell into it dead and so were directly buried in. The event is the real core of your play.

It is, by the way, an example of what I mean by site: the Germans had come along and found a piece of geography, a natural landscape that was designed for a massacre. The play begins in the average world of the kitchen table and not with Babi Yar, and I called the scenes 'houses' to suggest to the audience: 'All of this is happening in your house. Babi Yar is a consequence of your "*houseness*".' Nold's house really stands on the cliff in Babi Yar. Just as Nold is a soldier, but since a soldier is a human being I show him to begin with as an ordinary person dealing with the existential problems of living. The situation of this guy just happens to be a war. The play will have him studying for his life and ask: will he be corrupt or not?

'Someone' who comes to corrupt him at home is Gregory. He first appears in the same way as the Woman in At The Inland Sea*: he is a ghostly unreal sleepwalking vagrant, trespassing into Nold's normality – in the middle of his studying. But later on in the play, Gregory will be his very real sergeant on the cliff of Babi Yar. Who is he, really, to be such a corrupting and changing character?*

Gregory's is this ideological interpretation of reality, that the world is made out of the good and the bad and the bad would have to be destroyed by the good, and that if the good can destroy enough bad, then society will be good. He believes the world is a 'brick desert', a sewer, and he sees himself as a broken bottle. He probably became a sergeant to control the chaos and so he organizes things and he confronts Nold. He tells him not to try to learn about society and the world, and that in order to survive he has to let himself be corrupt to become a killer and not be killed. Nold may have created Gregory – or he may exist as a reality he would like to avoid. He is a sort of father, who looks at the education of his son. He represents authority, wisdom, what Virgil is to Dante – and he will be his guide in hell. Anyway, Nold is haunted by Gregory because he needs him to face himself, to create himself. Gregory is actually him as he could become twenty, thirty or fifty years after, if he can't open and observe the ambiguities of his life.

You said the starting point of your play is a detail in the account by one of the surviving victims of the Babi Yar massacre: she noticed the soldiers standing with their machine guns on the cliff on the other side of the ravine, taking a break to make coffee, as any employee would.

Yes, they were making coffee because they thought they had finished killing for the day and could relax after their day's work. But then they were told there was another batch of people to be shot. What impressed me was that a soldier threw his coffee away in disgust – not that he had to kill more people but that his free time was taken from him. And this guy was not joking – he was very upset that he couldn't drink his coffee in peace.

Your point is that these things cannot fit together: the inhumanity of the mass murder and in the same man the simple basic feeling of justice that he deserves his coffee for his hard work?

Yes: how can they occupy the same world? How could these guys make coffee in such a place? There, instead of the extraordinary coming inside normality, as in *At The Inland Sea,* or in Nold's house at the beginning of the play, the normality is inside an extraordinary situation. Making the coffee is an image of everyday life, a life on the surface, unconscious of the horror that stands behind the normality. This should be shocking – as it shocks Liz in *A Window.* It is true but frightening that in this world where we drink coffee there should also be Auschwitz. That is why you cannot get used to Auschwitz or to the accounts of Hiroshima, because they join together the colossal with the mundane and the ordinary. When I read this story I wondered why it was not the most famous story in human history. It seemed to be the key to the twentieth century. As much as this story by Primo Levi: when he was in Auschwitz he asked a kapo: 'Warum?' – Why? And the kapo answers: 'Hier ist kein warum!' – Here there is no why! But I think the Babi Yar story is more telling because there is not the expected poor prisoner and the brutal guard, only the soldier who wants his coffee and a heap of dead bodies. That horror of the coffee is more disturbing to face than the horror of Hiroshima and the death camps because it is about the perpetrators and not the victims. This creates a disturbance of meaning, it severs reason and emotion, it rips the ideological bind. It exemplifies Hannah Arendt's idea of the 'banality of evil': nothing is more banal than a coffee cup – but evil is the least banal of things. But my Babi Yar story is more profound because it doesn't concern Eichmann who watches hell through the office window but soldiers in the midst of it. It also includes the cosmos: this cliff could be an image of the edge of the universe on which stands the kitchen table where the soldier would have his coffee.

The central scene of the play you called 'The Big Ditch' happens precisely on the top of the cliff of Babi Yar – though you demand it to be set as a contemporary scene. How have you enacted the event in that scene?

The scene presents many sites in the same time. They are all necessary because we really exist on these different sites. Three different places are put on stage, as if separated by transparent screens. The first one is downstage and it is the little campaign canteen where the coffee is made.

It belongs to one of the soldiers who is in charge of the coffee. He sits apart from the others and doesn't take part in the shooting.

He has his own spot where he can have a talk behind the backs of the others. He is like someone keeping the refreshment stall during a football match. He doesn't really notice the game because he has his job to do and he has to be ready on time for the rush at the break – but when there is a goal or rummage in the spectators he looks at what is happening. His involvement in the scene is to show that the coffee is more important than the massacre. The most telling image is when, at the height of the firing, he stands behind the soldiers, holding their cups and having small gulps from these. He is only interested in his little spoils and not in the orgy of blood happening on the cliff over there.

In the scene he is the one who throws the coffee away.

It is provocative like a sulky kid who throws his shoes away because he has been ordered to put them on. When he does it he produces a silence around him: nobody knows how to react to it. The sergeant, Gregory, doesn't understand either. He is proud to show such liberality as to offer good coffee to his men and he takes this act as defiance. Then another soldier complains at the physical pain he has from his job – sitting at a machine gun all day. They are not annoyed by having to kill people, or by the suffering of their victims, but only that the work it requires is tiring – and ironically it isn't even about exhausting work, but only sitting. So the coffee thrown away is at the centre of the play, both structurally and analytically – the stillness at the centre of the tornado. It points to the fact that the soldiers only see their own petty vexations and don't have any understanding of their true situation.

This is also what we see of them when they are doing their dirty work.

This is the second place: the soldiers are upstage, on the top of the cliff facing the ravine that is out of sight for the audience and shooting over it at their victims. They release violence without having the slightest moment of reflection – just as soldiers during a battle don't think of the stupidity of war. It is important that the actors enact the absolute violence of the scene. They want to finish quickly with their extra job and drink their coffee in peace. They have no pity for the people they kill and never think they are human beings – at the most they hate them because they are delaying their coffee.

However, the scene is not routine for them because you introduce an incident that turns the experience of the soldiers upside down. They are used to shooting people mechanically with machine guns and they would just drop dead, but on this day they have run out of ammunition. So they have to use their rifles and kill them one by one, and this requires them to really look at them.

Because they are acting in this unusual way they are immersed in the operation, its steps and its consequences, and they face the dislocation of their normality – and so does the audience. They notice for the first time what they are doing or, more exactly, the soldiers actually *see* what the victims are doing when they shoot at them, which is usually caught up in their ordinary job. But they don't understand it either. They keep saying: 'Look at these people: isn't that odd? Why is this man with the coat falling in such a silly way? Why is he doing tricks with a rope?' and so on. They need to describe these extraordinary things because they are strange and new to them. They describe what they see at the very moment it happens, with a huge precision because it is very much unusual. They are like football supporters who would describe a player running closer to the goal – and like them they aren't interested in the meaning of the game, they just want to win. Or they could be like people shooting at dolls at the fair and hoping to gain a lot of money. Sometimes it even stops them. At one moment there is a silence in the middle of the shooting, as if they were seeing something unbelievable, like a miracle. They had a rolling fire, they killed everyone, except a girl who seems to be floating on her own in the air – like the holy Virgin during the Assumption? All they see is sheer reality, but they have the strangeness of things you are not used to seeing that suddenly appear, so they obviously translate it into a religious imagery of sufferings, martyrdom and miracles. They see all this as a series of events, each of them with its peculiarities, its purpose and its characteristics. It is important for the actors to play each step and not to generalize into chaos because of the cruelty and the frenzy of violence. Their actions and lines are always connected with a specific image or incident the soldiers actually see and experience and their violence is structured, controlled, by their comments and descriptions of it.

Audiences will never see their victims on the opposite cliff.

No, they won't. This is the third place of the scene, further beyond and unseen. It exposes the actual human meaning of this violence: the physical suffering, terror and death of the victims. It is important that we can't see it, because it reproduces the blindness of the audience – so that their job should be to imagine in their mind what is being described by the soldiers. Since imagination is involved – both the soldiers' and the audience's – this place is full of meanings, of interpretations of existence by the imagination. So the site is made out of these three places: the small spot for the coffee, which represents everyday life

– making the coffee, gossiping; the place where the soldiers do their job without thinking of what they are doing, which expresses what is involved in the life of the first place and gives it its meaning – say, for instance, the exploitation and sufferings of the Africans our affluence is based on; and the place where it all results in death and suffering, but that we only have to imagine. These places are gathered inside us in our everyday life, but they usually remain hidden one to the other – we only see the coffee place: the kitchen table. That is why on stage it has to exist for itself. The scene puts these layers of existence together, and makes them transparent – and the coffee machine is ticking like a heartbeat, though the soldiers are themselves heartless. We feel that there is no understanding on the top of that cliff – so that we can accept the responsibility, and also the *need* to change. It is *because* the soldiers don't understand that *we* have to understand what is happening there.

What do you do for the audience to understand this in that way?

I alter the sites – and this is disturbing. The reality we live in every day only exists in that form because the sites are carefully arranged and stacked by ideology. In drama we can change this arrangement of the sites – that is the whole point of it – by creating sites which are determinant and critical. This play is a constant process of learning for Nold – and whenever you learn something you have to relate to that segment of the mind to do with what you don't know, that is when you were an infant and had to learn very basic things: the very first state of human beings that I call the monad. Of course we cannot enter the mental world of the infant. It is forever lost to us, but it remains in us forever as the basis of all our further selves and we need a dramatic access to it. So before the play sends Nold to Babi Yar it puts him in this situation where the basic patterns of human self and society appear: what determines you as you are becoming human, how the self will experience reality and its place in it, how society allows you to live, what it makes you think and so on. All problems that have to be met and solved to become human. And this shows what will make possible what happens later, on the cliff of Babi Yar. It is like opening the situation to see what is involved in it – or like looking at it through a microscope which could show together the two dimensions: the edge of the universe and the kitchen table.

THE KITCHEN TABLE AND THE EDGE OF THE UNIVERSE

This happens at the very beginning of the play; as soon as Nold leaves his house to follow Gregory, he arrives in a mysterious, dark, unknown forest, where physical references become confused. Time and space seem to be moving (days pass by in minutes, the world outside can disappear or become very close), paths are erased, actions are contradictory, people can vanish in holes or get out elsewhere, or be transformed. Strange people live here, unexpected things happen. What is this enigmatic place about?

This part of the play is set in the world of imagination because this is how the infant experiences its relationship with the material world and this is what makes us human. Imagination comes from looking at reality and it tells you what you can't understand by conventional social logic – the imagination of adults in society is twisted and distorted by ideology to misunderstand this. The scene is an account of the way imagination is created and works and obeys its logic, which has nothing to do with fantasy but is firmly related to reality.

Is it a sort of reversion to the imagination of Nold as a child, as he is building himself as the adult person he will be in Babi Yar, to look at where it started from?

No it isn't. It shows the imagination as it is in the adult. The human mind lives in different times at once – the child is always there so that, in part, we understand our adult world as a child. This is the basis of creativity – but at its worst the imagination is imprisoned in ideology. Adults never face any problem that they have not already faced as a child in its rawest form. This is the humanness of our imagination. So there, Nold's experience is slotted into the creativity, the vividness, of the child's imagination. At the opening of the play, you see him, as a grown up, in the material world, in his house, and the world of imagination comes in and brings him to the 'Second House', the forest. There, you see how desires are pushed to their extreme and these extremes are supporting everyday life. It seems to be like in a sort of fairy tale, where kids get lost in the forest where a wicked witch lives and they have strange tasks to perform – but it is also Dante's forest which stands in the middle of existence and hides the door to hell. In it I created various totems: a Mother and a Father (that is Gregory, who, here, is like an ogre), a Boy

(Nold) and a Girl. All of them are negotiating their relationship to find how they could balance the human mind – Nold's mind in this case, because it is happening in his head – and sort out its reality so that it would become viable for him. This means to know what is happening in him in relation to what is happening outside. All these are social relationships involved in a personal situation, Nold's.

How do they concretely act in the play to make these relationships visible?

You see Gregory and the Woman (the 'mother') fighting each other and asking Nold to agree with them as if they were competing for the meaning of reality. Gregory tells Nold this place is his – at this point, he is telling him he has a right to be in the world – and the Woman will try to drag him out. The Woman with the Girl shows what a motherly relationship is: she comforts her, makes her daughter endure hunger and threats or cope with her own fears and hopes. We see how this relationship produces humanness – the human passion can be expressed in the very gentle act of washing hands. They also have a picnic in which the Woman performs all the customs and manners of the table and the Girl tries to interpret the meaning of these gestures and guess how to respond to them. It is all very practical but it unconsciously involves the whole of behaviour in society. The Girl is not fully mentally aware, she is like a baby. She really is this aspect of Nold which has to learn, and she lives both in fear and joy towards the unknown. She is in the position of always being born. She constantly uses her imagination to search for the meaning of what she sees and experiences by producing images. She seems to be looking at the question of the world outside the world of things and immediate desire (where she has to eat and so on) with great clarity and with no panic. But for her it is an absolutely practical process: the images are very direct, they are a form of knowledge in themselves, they don't need to be interpreted but seen – words only remind us what we know when we look at the sky, the stones, the mice and organize these in a story. The Girl exemplifies what I just described about the way imagination works. And Nold observes her trying to learn how to organize her life, grow and be an adult.

THE KITCHEN TABLE AND THE EDGE OF THE UNIVERSE

The Woman and the Girl live in an absolute destitution; they inhabit a sort of lair and they are in a state of everlasting starvation. Nold does everything he can to help them; he tries to go back home to bring them food but he desperately can't find his way out of the forest.

Nold thinks he can change the world. In all the darkness and confusion of the forest, and its changing realities, the only permanent feature is Nold's absolute, desperate and active desire to do good. But he finds himself exposed – as if he were a passenger in a plane, and suddenly the plane is not there any more. He thinks he knows how to help the women, but he discovers that wisdom is ignorance, authority is impotency: he has to accept responsibility. He is faced with the limits of his power in an unjust world. It is the immediacy of the child-mind in the adult-prison.

This is shown by the fact that in spite of his efforts, the Woman ends by killing her daughter because she can't control her suffering any more.

Her decision to kill her comes directly from Nold's attempts to do good. The Woman doesn't believe he will manage – the play shows him failing twice. She notices this raises wild hopes in the Girl and when she sees how exited she gets so that she sets up a picnic as a welcoming feast for his return (because the Girl now considers Nold as her hero), the Woman understands the Girl could never bear the disappointment when he comes back (if he ever does) empty-handed. The Woman was ready to fight and to beg to keep her alive and safe but this time she loses hope. She considers this as a mercy killing; she intends to spare the Girl the torments of hunger and the suffering of being in the world – it is an act of resistance against the suffering of the world. This is the ultimate contradiction: she kills her daughter out of love. As a further contradiction, another 'trick' from the forest, Nold comes back just precisely then, as the Woman said he never would – then all the contradictions active in the scene are clearly, almost schematically, presented.

Nold will wrongly blame Gregory for the death of the Girl, he rages against him and wants to kill him – whereas the Woman meanwhile has just vanished.

His consuming anger for his failure changes him, turns him into a killer. These are adult passions, as children live them: serious, tragic, cosmically comic – and that makes us human. So in the forest Nold goes through the critical stages of growing up to be an adult, then the play transfers the problem into the social situation, and what was potential takes part in it. The structures created in the forest are replaced by a social, physical order and the basic human patterns exposed in it are now set in historical circumstances: Babi Yar. Then the question isn't: 'Is there such thing as a good SS man who will save the women?' but: 'What is human or potentially human in people involved in that situation?'

This reversal is very disturbing because all of a sudden, Nold appears as a member of the killing squad in Babi Yar and he seems to have no connexion any more with this story in the forest and its characters. Soon we will see Gregory as his sergeant and we will attend the killing scene we have been discussing earlier on. Is the play back to reality after a diversion then?

Let's call the scene at the top of the cliff 'factual'; it is a fact that happens – and it is all the more real that it is a genuine historical incident and it takes place as it happened to a real person during the historical Babi Yar massacre. You would think the world of reality should be freed from the contradictions of the forest, but it isn't. In the Big Ditch the contradictions of the forest become real, as if imagination were bleeding a black blood in the real world. But this is Babi Yar that should be imaginary, a vicious phantasm – but it isn't. It is as if as adults we live in the fictions we no longer understand – this is the corruption of the child that society demands.

Yes, I think this really is the real point: Babi Yar is so extraordinary (literally: out of the usual standards of normality) that it makes the relationship between imagination and reality critical and questionable. And then it is so obviously inhumanly monstrous that you can only reject it with disgust, but this doesn't allow you to understand anything of it. Is this the reason why you designed this complex structure for the play?

Exactly. The problem of the play is: 'How do you relate those two worlds and where do you accept responsibility?' The drama opens the processes in Nold in the Second House – which you usually can't do because society represses it. If the play had gone immediately to Babi Yar (say it begins when a postman arrives at Nold's and gives him a formal army travel warrant), audiences would have been much more able conventionally to cope with that. They would have thought: 'Yes, Babi Yar was bad, we must think about it …' And if the forest would have come after the 'Big Ditch', they would have thought: 'Yes, we are thinking about Babi Yar now.' *Nothing* much would have been gained because they couldn't ask themselves, how did we get there? As the forest scene comes first, it seems a nice mystery story where you wonder: 'Who is who? Who is this strange figure that keeps appearing? What can be the key to the story?' Audiences can easily identify with it in their imagination, as if they were reading *Alice in Wonderland*, and be happy about that … But they won't end by waking up from a dream – instead of that, they will arrive in Babi Yar. This means not that *they* (the characters) have a problem, but *we* (the audience) have a problem. Since they could follow what was happening in the forest, they can then go to Babi Yar, find themselves there, in the middle of history and wonder by which hell of a path they happened to have got there. What is disturbing is that instead of watching this fantasy picnic in the forest we now see soldiers making coffee and that isn't a fantasy, that is what you do in real life and did in history. So the question becomes: 'How does this relate to us?' *We* are there, now, and we have to ask ourselves which side of the canyon are we on: the killer's or the victim's? But because of the way the drama is constructed, the audience don't ask the question, the question questions them.

The play will perform then another reversal. After the killing scene on the top of the cliff, it brings us directly to the bottom of the ravine, turned into a mass grave, literally among the dead. There, we meet again the women of the forest, who were among the victims but were not killed, and Nold comes face to face with them. They don't recognize each other, but Nold becomes suddenly unable to kill them, as he is ordered to by Gregory.

We change the site again: we go down *into* Babi Yar and this is the 'Third House'. The forest and the Big Ditch come together as one site to elucidate their relationships. It is as if the Big Ditch scene had been a tsunami of blood, bullets, violence, coffee, hysteria and that now the tide that overwhelmed that world had left and people can look at the disaster around them. It is only then that the reflection comes to the soldiers – and only one of them, Nold, because *he* realizes what he is doing. Even then he would have to dig deep inside himself to find out the consequences of this – and this is hard and requires him to know himself in terms of the forest.

How can he do that since none of the characters remembers or takes into account what they have been experiencing in the forest?

They do it on a more basic ground because they are always in the Second House, but they don't know it objectively – if they did it wouldn't work, it could just be childhood fantasy. Instead, it has to be built into the present, integrate into it. They try to remember these experiences, to understand what they are doing here – or they turn their back on it in fear. The world of darkness and imagination exposed in the forest is buried in the Big Ditch as well as in this Third House, and it goes on haunting the whole play. And it really affects it.

In what way?

For instance, you can see nothing happens as it should for the soldiers, until eventually, when they go down in the ditch, the women reappear and Nold is unable to shoot any more. The pictures appearing in the forest are developing throughout the play, like waves provoked by a pebble in the water – sometimes they appear like a tidal wave or an erupting volcano. The characters too behave according to the same patterns they followed in the forest. You see the women performing again strange actions, to confront the soldiers and to try to save their lives. For example, the mother tries to distract her daughter from the killers and pretends to be a boat by opening her coat – and the wind turns it into a sail and her daughter puts a rope she took from a dead body on her to achieve the image. Gregory wants them dead, as he did when he was the ogre in the forest, and he tries to persuade, coerce, seduce Nold into killing them now in the Big Ditch. If he does, it would prove to Gregory that he is right about reality. He tells Nold about being at home and shows family photographs and reminds him they are all pals together and so on. He praises the normal world, the world *we* are living in and this is a world that is able to accept Babi Yar, that is the foundation of Babi Yar, just as Xenia in *Summer* is the foundation of the killings on the island. Gregory is telling Nold not to ask questions about society or the world. Then the question is really to the audience: 'What world are you in? Where is your world leading you to? What is it the basis of?'

Why wouldn't Nold listen to him and obey him any more?

Nold does listen to Gregory but he opposes him with his innocence: he refuses to kill the women, just because there is no reason why he should do such a thing. Nold and Gregory are disputing the meaning of human reality. For Nold this is a battle to become human. Then the scene is not so much about giving orders, obey or disobey them, but about taking the responsibility for the whole human species.

The battle is not only between Gregory and Nold. The Woman is involved in it too and she confronts the soldiers to try to make them spare her daughter.

That is right. At one moment, she faces the soldiers, stands against them and offers herself to be shot instead of her daughter. She opens her coat widely and becomes a *niké* (really like the Victory of Samothrace in the Louvre), an image of freedom. Then she will keep confronting her killers with freedom and the whole physicality of the actress should keep suggesting this gesture. When after that her daughter is taken away from her to be shot, she raises her finger and claims: 'This space is mine – the space between my finger and my daughter is mine.' She doesn't point: she tries to touch her daughter who is out of reach. The way she stretches her finger is the opposite of all military movements in the play that come from orders. The site seems to be owned by the killers who have the power of the gun – the thing – and give instructions. But she says she owns this space that relates her to her daughter. It is her site because she can have this human claim on it – and the soldiers don't know it. So she can know – and she says so – that in this space the dead could stand up and walk away from the soldiers who killed them if they could know what this space is, but her miracle is that as she can now claim this space is hers there will be a time when soldiers can't kill on it – because the power of humanness is greater than the power of destructiveness. And in the middle of this hell, there is a place of life. Because she has the understanding of that moment, of her reason to live now, the reality is hers. This line is like a signpost pointing down at our feet which says: 'This is here' – all the suffering of the world is here, and *here* she can denounce this extreme destruction. In Alain Françon's production of the play in Paris, the actress playing that part, Dominique Valadié, took several steps as if it actually was her space. It was extraordinary. She had the authority of that moment.

This has a critical effect on Nold because he immediately kills Gregory instead of the women. He eliminates the authority and escapes with the Girl to save her.

The Woman's attitude in the scene has been announcing this. Now something new will happen, something more powerful than the 'miracle' she performed, it will be a *human* miracle: Nold will kill Gregory. Nold in the end, as a tragic hero, by his action, takes the responsibility of the moment. As the Woman's finger draws a new space, Nold's finger feels the trigger and is about to make a new world possible. It is a human being breaking the rules. In the forest, the Woman killed an innocent – now, Nold kills the guilty one.

How can we figure out the general pattern designed by the sites on the comprehensive scale of the play? Can we consider they are all contained inside Babi Yar?

Babi Yar is also in the forest scene. That is the whole point: sites are like Russian dolls, one inside the other. Nold is in the Third House and in the Second House. And so is the audience – that is the importance of drama. All the 'houses' are really happening in the same time, they are here together, like the four sides of a square – with a mass grave in its centre. Each world has its own reality but they are all connected. The play intends to be a complete map of a specific human reality and so this involves Nold in a process during which he discovers (or

THE KITCHEN TABLE AND THE EDGE OF THE UNIVERSE

better, he creates) his personal self. In that sense, I make him behave according to what I think being human is about. So the play looks at all the problematic of being human – but you still have to get up in the morning. That is why at the end we see Nold sitting at a kitchen table once again but this is now in a house – the 'Fourth House' – that stands in a bombed city.

8
REALITY DOESN'T BECOME PRACTICAL UNTIL IT TELLS YOU ITS MEANING

Born: imagination X-rays reality / *Chair*: all Billy can do is to imagine / *Have I None*: the imagination outlaw / I use sleep in the way Shakespeare used ghosts / The sleepwalking WAPO / Peter has never been resisting / Donna, the extremist nailed to the world / Luke is looking for the meaning of life, even among the dead / The Invisible Object.

After Coffee, *you kept developing and experimenting on this combination of various realities in your further plays, especially in* Born. *The first half of this play follows the linear development of a story: we first see a couple, Donna and Peter, moving into a new home with their baby, Luke. Then twenty years after, society has collapsed and they are being deported into camps by the 'war police', the 'WAPOS', in which Luke has become an officer. Then we follow Luke's deeds with his squad. But halfway through the play, this plot seems to twist: the second part of the play brings us back to the house of the beginning which Luke had transformed into a death camp for his squad, and that is now full of dead bodies. But the place has become a very uncertain site where what happens cannot be read in realistic narrative terms any more: the characters do or do not recognize each other, their behaviour can change quickly, and we will even see the dead rising!*

This last scene is like an X-ray of the everyday life we saw in the first scene when Donna and Peter moved into their new home. It shows what is behind it by reusing its basic elements. For instance, we saw them carrying the table with baby Luke lying on it to the window, which was half-covered by a curtain – to prevent the neighbours from seeing inside. They had just had their first meal on this table and it was then very easy to move. In the last scene, in the middle of the dead, we see Luke as an adult starving and crawling on the floor, desperately trying to reach a bowl of food on the table by toppling it – and he eventually breaks the bowl and there is no food in it. After that, we see the father himself turned into a WAPO, ordering the dead with extreme violence to move the table to the window, which has now been completely closed by a sheet of iron. The table is then extremely difficult to move and this involves huge violence and terror so that it evokes slave labour in a concentration camp. The table has become so heavy because we do not organize society properly and now we have to deploy enormous efforts to accomplish something which should be simple. You should have foreseen that and acted on that because beyond what you are immediately doing, you are doing something to the world. We should take responsibility for our lives and to do that we must first understand them. I am not saying that by moving the table you open a concentration camp – like a distant butterfly-effect – but that the life you lead results in a concentration camp. Our present social situation has become an enormous burden, a dead weight on human society. In dramatic terms, the weight will press out something in the psychology of the self.

Does the scene take place in the imagination in the way the forest scene did in Coffee?

Not really. In *Coffee*, the forest is the site of imagination and it lies – invisibly – behind the reality site at the bottom of the ditch. For *Born*, I put both on stage at the same time, as one site: what the fiction assumes as the real and what Luke experiences in his imagination – but the other characters also bring their own realities into it. The play asserts that all these realities are one and here it pushes the imaginary a bit further and enacts it. So it is very difficult to say what the stage reality of that moment in the scene is.

REALITY DOESN'T BECOME PRACTICAL

Let's take the things from the beginning, then. Peter is trying to rescue Luke who, after some misadventures, has been left for dead in a no man's land and brings him back to the house.

This is a realistic action (and Peter uses a very ordinary kitchen chair to carry Luke on his back). They come from a degenerate ruined world, bombed, shelled, laid waste: the real world outside. But Donna is already in the house, living in another reality in her imagination where she can nurse and feed the dead because she believes they need it. The dead are there for real and they don't react to what Donna does to them – but when, later on, the dead rise, they are ghosts in Luke's imagination. Earlier, when her husband and son return to the house, Donna doesn't recognize them: have they become objects in her imagination? Is all this happening in her imagination? Or Luke's? Or Peter's? It is as if the world is dozing: it is half awake, half asleep and it can cross the border of sleep and consciousness. These events are not fantasy: they perform the logic of reality. The scene compounds reality so that you see the consequences of what you are doing immediately. It is a synoptic involvement in reality.

You are making there a different use of the imagination than in Coffee's *forest, then. It is not so much about looking inside imagination at the structures of reality or the roots of what is happening in the real practical world, than about reading reality in imagination terms. But what do we get from this double level reading?*

This is what human reality is all about. We live and understand reality in imaginary ways and much of our reality is fiction. We actually *live* in the interaction between these two worlds: the material world and the world of imagination. The first exists only because the second perceives it – the second only exists according to the first. You can have nothing in your head that is not first in the world – I believe this as an article of faith: there is nothing supernatural in existence. But reality doesn't become practical until it tells you its meaning. This means that to understand anything, I need reason *and* imagination: reason to know the causes and imagination to understand the meaning. Any event happening to anybody is given its meaning within their subjective self – so that human reality is a passage between the subjective and the objective. So any object is also in your head if it is on the table: we both *receive* the world from outside and *project* the world from inside. Imagination is a language that can speak backwards and forwards. The logic of imagination is not to provide an escape from reality but to show us how we are attached to reality.

Could this be seen in an experimental way in Billy's situation in Chair? *In this sense that Billy is a boy who grew up inside an apartment without any contact with the outside world – he was found as an abandoned baby in the street by a woman who since then kept him hidden from a criminal totalitarian state that would certainly destroy him. So he doesn't know reality but only what he figures it out to be in his imagination – and the play allows us to see this through his drawings.*

Yes. Billy has only seen the real world from the window – and not even too much because he mustn't be seen from the outside and it is anyway frightening. He seeks to understand what happens beyond the window but all he can do is to imagine and he puts the realities he invented on paper – which has itself the shape of a window. If he wants something to happen, or to know something, he just draws it and tells its story – like a very primitive form of magic. So Billy is drawing everywhere, all the time, and his drawings cover all the walls of the room and create the reality in which he lives. Drawing is his way of life. Through the drawings and the stories he tells about them, he can control the events in a way he can't in reality. He takes everything from reality and transforms it so that it enters his imaginary world – and he tends to make reality good because he needs to be reassured. So the drawings are not a way of escaping from reality, but a way of asking for the meaning of things, and finding the truth of the situation. Notice for instance he doesn't just invent names for the people he draws: he waits until he knows their real name. When he tells his story of the man who walked on the ocean to reach the end of the world – who is obviously himself – he can call him 'Mr Dot' only at the end, after he found how to identify with it – a dot is something so small it almost doesn't exist in the immensity of space.

This is a long story and while Alice is outside in danger he draws many pictures about imaginary dangers – it is this scene with the chair and the old woman prisoner we already discussed. He tells her his story right away when she comes back because he is very satisfied with this work. What does the story mean for Billy?

His story deals with the external world he fears. At the moment he is afraid of what happens in the street. It describes a difficult world, with mountains, physical obstacles, a feeling of chaos. Walking on the water – as Mr Dot does in his drawings – is a way of controlling reality but unfortunately a storm comes in and erases Mr Dot's footsteps so that he is lost. It is as if through the story he was saying: 'I want to get out! I want to get out!' But in the end he says it is better not to. So you see the drawings are like a sign language which conveys what is happening inside him, but they also evoke the immediate situation as well as the general problems of life.

But what Billy's case would miss in order to exemplify this work of imagination as you described it would be the second part of the process: Billy can't put his imagination to the test by experiencing it back on reality.

No he can't. At the end of the play, Billy has to go out of his room, into the real world – and he finds himself as if he were inside his drawings – but he is unable to control it in the way he did before and this frightens him. When I was writing the play I wanted to enact this and I imagined – but eventually didn't do it – that he could pick up a pebble or a piece of chalk and start drawing on the pavement. Then he would hear a dog barking or the alarm of a police car, and he would run away because he would see his drawing method doesn't work any more. In the play, he ends up by being shot. But what you normally do when you are in a situation you don't know anything about, is to use your imagination to interpret it, not to pretend to monitor it from within yourself like Billy. I remember this image described by a soldier from the Falklands War – it was at the origins of my TV play *Tuesday*: he was on the top of a rocky hill which he said was 'like being in a room surrounded by rocks'. He was in a situation of life and death and talked about it as if it was the space he normally lived in – a room. When you are on the seaside and look at the ocean, you wouldn't say: 'This thing reminds me of my bathroom!' It would be the other way round. The soldier's life has been transferred into a different shape so that made him very conscious of what was happening to him and he could see things differently – so he could change. At least, this is what happens to the soldier in my play when he finds himself in this image.

In Have I None, *which is set in the same future as* Chair, *we see any human activity involving imagination strongly repressed by society as being a risk of disorder. But imagination seems to leak from people in spite of themselves and even against people's will.*

Yes. It is justified by the policeman in the play, Jams, in a tragic speech which sounds like the Grand Inquisitor in *The Brothers Karamazov* when he tells Christ: 'You came here and promised people freedom but what they really want is imprisonment so that they don't have to make any decisions: they are all made for them.' This society imposes such a discipline that people won't be conscious, they won't have to make any choices, they won't have any question – so that, Jams thinks, they won't suffer any more. So what the society in the play does is build the perfect prison. But even in a perfect prison dust keeps coming in the window … You could try to make sure the dust will be where you want it – but it won't be because the universe doesn't behave as you want it to. There is always a limit to what you can control – this is why dictatorships fail. The logic of that society is this: people are in prison – but they look out by the window. So they cover the window – but they see things on the wall. So they turn off the light – but some people can see in the dark. So they blind them – but they can have visions in their head. So they kill them, so that their lives can be perfect.

In the play when people are faced with a problem, they just don't know how to deal with it: they can't decently imagine what to do, they can only foresee the worst and they immediately panic.

Everything has its exact place – like the gaffer tape the stage manager puts on stage to mark the place of the props and sets for the scene changes. So, if the chair is in its right place and the right person is sitting on it, then everything is in order. When a stranger moves a chair and sits on it, they panic and the universe is falling apart. Eventually things are really getting out of control: not only is the table in the wrong place, but it is coming apart. The situation is desperate and they decide they had better kill the stranger. It is a parodic example of the idea we have already discussed of putting the objects in the wrong place. The characters are obsessed with the place of things because authority has abolished the past and this made society amnesiac. No one knows where they are or where anything should have its natural customary place. So there has to be an order saying where everything is and should be. Everything enters the meaning of life that society dictates. This makes 'custom' pathologically rigid.

Eventually the only escape people have is to compulsively commit mass suicide, by waves, as if they were collectively sleepwalking – as if they were unconsciously monitored by their imagination.

By committing suicide, the people in the play are acting like those people in prison who deliberately wound themselves – as if their body was the prison and they were destroying it to get out, or they bang their head against the wall as if they could knock a hole in it and get out. They only manage to hurt themselves, of course. In the play they commit suicide not because they are fed up with life but because they want to live. But they are not allowed to live as they want and they should. They enact the reality of their social situation. One character saw people jumping off a bridge in a river and he says their coats blow up like big bubbles in the water inflated with their last breath. This is an image of humanness that can't be destroyed in that way – as if, in the end, air will invent a lung so it can be breathed.

In a way this is what happens to Sara in the play: there is nothing to imagine, but her imagination works nevertheless and so she imagines non-existent knocks on the door.

It is as if you could hear the wall cracking in the perfect prison – or the inmates knocking their heads. It seems something is knocking *there*, inside her head. This worries her, but like a pain in a tooth. When she tells her husband, Jams, about this knocking, it makes him very angry. He himself lives in unease because his job entails him patrolling a place of ruins inside the city where things and people forbidden in the streets are hidden. This is the repressed world (but not in a Freudian way) where the whole process of destruction of that society has been accomplished. A world somehow of the past like a ruined graveyard where the stones are old and all falling over, or a mausoleum inhabited by very old, strange and ancient people – like the old woman Jams saw standing on a table, we mentioned earlier. So he is in contact with a world exciting his imagination and he has to repress this all the time. It opens a dangerous area between him and authority and he can't cope with that.

Sara's hallucination continues until one day there actually is someone at the door claiming he is her brother – which is not possible.

But are they really brother and sister? I don't know – the question is much more interesting than the answer anyway … He comes like a messenger of life from another world far away beyond the city, that still has potential life in it, where the disaster is not yet fully accomplished. His clothes (an old fawn mac and a trilby) are an image of past life. He is real but he is also a figment of Sara's mind, she is inventing with various odds and ends, to create a human relationship which is forbidden by her society.

It develops further because later on, the brother will have his own fantasy in which he hears knocking at the door and Sara enters.

The play refines and develops its images and each of them now stands for their repressed – forbidden – human life. Sara is then wearing this blue coat covered with spoons like stars in the night sky – really: it has to be a random collection, not an ordered pattern but an image of disorganization and chaos, of the contingency of life. It is a diary of life through a record of meals. Then she tells her brother a childhood memory which is a sort of primal scene. They were in a dark house, he was sick and in danger of dying. She feared the doctor, who was like an ogre, would kill him and they were struggling to look out of the window and see outside the life they would grow up and go into. This memory, this story, is complex and so indecipherable – because it is about deciphering – that only children can understand it – and they do that perfectly. After the story, she gently puts the brother to sleep (which is an obvious image of death) and then turns the coat inside out so that you see the lining is covered with bones – because on this level, the process of living is also a process of dying. So, in the middle of the most regimented society you can imagine, there is a dream about the inefficiency of regimentation where everything changes naturally from one thing to the other and back again without the violence and the panic of that society.

You show by the way often your characters dreaming – as we have already mentioned for the Dummy in The Under Room. *They bear witness then from their inner imaginary world. How does this influence them when they wake?*

I use sleep in the way Shakespeare used ghosts who come in and say things that you usually couldn't. It is that Hamlet thing: 'There are more things in heaven and earth, Horatio / Than are dreamt of in your philosophy.' Letting a person do or say something when he is asleep opens to the part of him that is not rationally thinking and so to alternative possibilities in him. When it cannot clearly articulate the situation, thought escapes into sleep as if it withdrew into a safer place, where it is creative but not yet conscious. Imagination becomes active, and then the characters have an access to tragic reality they don't have when they are awake. They are moved by the tragic situation. My Medea, for instance – in this play I still haven't finished and which I first called *There Will be More* but now call *Dea* – murders her babies in a sort of sleep and when her husband Johnson asks her why, she keeps answering: 'Because you wanted me to do it.' It doesn't explain why she did it but in her dream she could perform the truth of her situation. In the material world you can always walk away from your situation and ignore reality for long periods. But not in imagination because it seeks reason and it always asks you: 'What do you do in that situation?' Imagination is more demanding than reality and in that way it can change reality.

In Born, *there is a dreamer who intervenes in reality in a very dramatic way: it is one of the WAPOS, WAPO 2. He not only sleeps, dreams and talks, he also sleepwalks and he manages, asleep, to grab hold of all the weapons of his pals and to spread panic among them by threatening to shoot at them.*

WAPO 2 is not fully integrated in the squad – he is like an octopus's leg that wouldn't really respond with the others. He doesn't like these people, although externally he is one of them – that is why they will eventually shoot him. When he is asleep, he is released from this tension because he is out of the pressures of the group. He is not afraid any more and his conscious conformity is no more operative. He goes into that world of dreams where he can enter into another dialogue with himself and he becomes the opposite of what he is when he is awake, that is, he becomes his true self. Then, he can truly re-examine the atrocities he participated in with the WAPOS and respond to it in a human way.

The chief of these atrocities you mentioned is this gruesome scene just before, when we saw the WAPOS ordered by their officer Luke to torment and eventually kill a Woman with her baby. This is the scene WAPO 2 is dreaming of now.

Yes, but note this is accompanied by a change of the site so that the landscape shows the changed psychology of the characters. The previous scene happened on a green hill like pastures, which seemed an ideal landscape of spring life – but the WAPOS turned it into a site of death by performing an atrocity there. It also referred to this Anglican hymn for children, that sings about Golgotha as 'a green hill far away without a city wall / Where our dear Lord was crucified / Who died to save us all'. In this scene, the site has become a grey stone dip, as if the Babi Yar cliff face in *Coffee* had been simplified and turned into a skull – a skull operating without a brain, seeking its own consciousness. I turn the coin round and look at the consequences of that violence in the psyche, the cost of human suffering involved in the collapsing society – not what they do to the victim, but what they have done (or has been done) to themselves.

And firstly in WAPO 2's mind through his dream. Nevertheless when as an audience we watched the scene, WAPO 2 participated in the action, and even seemed to do it quite joyfully.

But he has obviously been deeply disturbed by this scene. At that time, he has already shown some symptoms of vulnerability by doing unwillingly everything wrong – though he is usually a really competent soldier. He tried to control this by being comic and laughing at it – he still has something childlike. All the WAPOS were affected in their own way: WAPO 1, who was closely confronted by it because he was holding the Woman, only showed bad will – the others were moaning – or fought over nothing after it was finished. This is what will make them mutiny against Luke later on – but only because they conclude from his action he had gone crazy. Among them, only WAPO 2 does something against it and he can do that only because he is dreaming. It is only then that he can bear the tension and he acts out those impulses in himself that he repressed when the scene actually happened.

What effects does the dream have on him then?

He becomes very destructive and very frightening. In his dream he can understand what the Woman was experiencing – he reproduces the sound she made when her baby was killed – and he is the only one who noticed she bit one of their riot shields – in his dream he says his hand was bitten. And he responds to it. For instance during the scene, the WAPOS were tramping in unison – as they are trained to do before they charge in order to be menacing and to keep together as a unit. They do this when they hold their shields to form the wall that the baby is crushed against. In his dream, WAPO 2 uses this pattern against the organization and that part of himself which consented to be involved in the WAPOs' crimes when he was awake – against all that has been done to him so that he consents. He is tramping but it becomes solemn and grandiose: it is of a god marching but also of an infant learning to walk. He then collects all the guns and he keeps them as a child with all his toys gathered around him – and eventually his NCO will manage to control him by treating him like a child. But he also physically controls the stage and he patrols the horizon of the dip so that he becomes an image of fate – because what Luke did with the Woman and her baby was a transgression and, as in Greek tragedies, when something has been transgressed, fate comes and is threatening.

It is precisely then that the play changes nature. It seems that reality begins to go wrong as if stressed by another logic trying to take over: the plot is contaminated by a series of coincidences, characters have irrational thoughts or over-react, this army of killers is subjugated by a sleeping boy ... And all this will eventually result in this last imaginary scene in the house that we started to talk about.

Chance becomes a decisive factor in the scene and this shows that the characters are about to confront deeper truths in the tragic situation. It really is the appearance of the hidden inevitability – like a Sophoclean irony. You can ask why Oedipus met Laius on the crossroad – if he didn't he would have bumped into him on his doorstep or anywhere. What happens as chance is in fact the working of the logic of imagination in the situation, as if reality itself were plotting so that things happen that can solve its problems. This is possible in drama, because it is a special sort of reality: it is a reality within a reality taking up its problems into such a situation that we can examine them, in the guise of fiction, as if they weren't part of reality. That is what drama does: it makes the audience's imagination face the problems they have in the reality of their lives. It deals with the reality in the audience's mind. But not so that they ask themselves: 'What shall I do in this situation?' – that is what you ask yourself in reality and what the characters in the play ask themselves – but: 'What is the meaning of reality? What does reality want to do?' As if drama itself were the consciousness of reality.

And what happens precisely there, in Born *(to come back to it), is that Luke, against all odds, is suddenly confronted by his father, who, without realizing who he is, first tries to kill him, as the WAPOS ordered him to, and then to save him.*

Luke was actively involved in questioning the nature of life – but he was really asking himself why he is a WAPO. And what he finds out is his father as an image of power as part of the elemental relationships that are the foundation of being human. When they realize that, all the WAPOS run away in fear. They won't face the problem – but Luke does.

This confrontation brings Luke, carried on his father's back, directly to the house full of the dead his mother is trying to nurse and feed – for the last scene that is dominated by the imagination, that we have already talked about for some time. How is the development of the characters affected by this dimension of the imaginary?

REALITY DOESN'T BECOME PRACTICAL

The three main characters remain the same as they were in the previous scenes. They don't change but they have here an ontological dimension, they show what essentially they are. The father, for instance, Peter, in the beginning is a very ordinary person. He is a nice guy – maybe too nice, too indulging. He is always compromising with everything, he never resists. In the first scene, he faces only the limited and commercial authority of the removal men. Well, they clearly haven't been doing their job properly – they broke things and want to leave early and want Peter to sign 'everything satisfactory' on the form. But he accepts this and says there is no problem. In the next scene, Peter and Donna are deported by the WAPOS. Authority is now political and more violent and Peter is still acquiescing, until we see him totally reduced to impotence: he sits in his house, holding a hammer he doesn't use, as the WAPOS led by his own son take over with their gear and weapons and they just ignore him. You can see Peter's attitude isn't constructive, it is only a form of assent. A quietest pacifist life is a sham because in reality violence will not just submit to it. Inside this indulgence lies in fact a great violence. This is what the last scene with the dead reveals: we see Peter coming back as a WAPO and, as I have already described, he forces the dead and drives them to work, very violently, kicking them and firing at them, like the Commandant of a concentration camp. He is consumed by revenge. He hasn't been resisting the WAPO in himself either. His wife, Donna, is the opposite. She is very conscious of standing on her own human right and doesn't let herself be manipulated. She blames Peter for his attitude to the removal men and when she is confronted with deportation, she refuses to obey – whereas Peter tries to convince her to. She is a mother in that she has to be practical, feed and provide – but she also has ideals: in the first scene she serves the meal and makes plans for a better home and so on. Then she will strongly reject the society ruled by the WAPOS. During the deportation scene, she stubbornly refuses to co-operate and would try to find an alternative and since she can't, she believes Luke must be joining some resistance group somewhere.

She briefly meets him then and it is clear from his attitude he won't join the deportees – but she doesn't know that he has joined the WAPOS, so she misunderstands his intentions.

Yes. Then she has a visionary speech: she holds out her arms towards him with her eyes shut, and she imagines he will escape and change the world. To allow him to go into hiding with no remorse about abandoning his parents, she wants to erase herself. She says: 'Don't think of me, I'm dead', and with this she gives him his life. But also, as a practical woman and a loving mother, she builds with her imagination her own means of surviving the parting from her son. First, she wants to keep something of him nobody could take away from her – so she remembers him when he was a little boy as only she knew him. But this is painful, so she erases this picture by saying her son is just any boy, now, so as in this way to make him a complete stranger. Then she can say she never saw him before – and by then Luke has physically left the stage. He enacted what she imagined, but with the opposite meaning – this is the human complexity. So you see, in her speech, Donna isn't trying to escape from the situation but to find the means to face it. Very practically, step by step, she managed to control reality by her imagination and she built a world where she could bear to lose her son. This reveals that though she tends towards an ideal, it is not just wishful thinking: she accepts that she must pay the cost of the extreme. This is what makes her a real extremist.

In the last scene we will see her keeping to such a titanic and completely illusory task as feeding and nursing the dead to prevent them from suffering.

It comes from this speech. She cannot bear that other people can be inhuman so eventually the thought of other people's suffering, their deadness, all they endured before they died, is unbearable. It is more profound than a moral feeling, it touches on her reason: for her it is intellectually offensive. She has to do something about it. So she nurses the people killed by Luke and the WAPOS, in order to keep them alive – just as she would have with her baby in the first scene. She isn't only a mother looking after her own child. She becomes an archetypal figure of a mother nursing the world with such extreme compassion that she cares only for the weakest and the most needy, that is: the dead. She treats them as children, but still in a practical way – she says: 'Do your button up. Be clean. Do this. Do that.' Her attitude is a total immersion in all the dimensions of the present and this involvement has taken her over completely. She constantly has this determination, as if she was

REALITY DOESN'T BECOME PRACTICAL

pushing something forward. She believes if she can feed these dead people and keep them alive she is saving the world, healing its pain, putting it in order. Her love keeps the world alive.

But all this is an illusion she creates for herself, it doesn't work for long.

This gives her a home she could be busy in. It is easier to live with the dead than with the living, because the living have questions she cannot answer whereas the dead have no questions, only starvation – and they will always do what they are told. At the end of the scene, she realizes the dead are not eating the food she gives them as if they were refusing to play this game any more. So she becomes desperate. She talks about her motives and herself because she has no way of evacuating the pain outside herself. She has nothing else to offer but her own suffering – crying is still an expression of love, desire, sorrow. She wants to find the last crumb in the world that could heal their pain and save the world. But when she finds it the dead won't eat this crumb either, so she will eat it for them. This is an obvious Eucharistic image and she turns it into a crucifixion image: as she can't eat the crumb it becomes a nail, nailing her on the world. The human suffering is so great that to walk on earth is for her to be crucified on it.

What about their son Luke, then?

In Luke the characteristics of both his parents come together in a sort of negative resolution. His human side is paralysed because he has been taken over by the WAPO-society – just as we saw the WAPOS physically turning the apartment into their death camp. He is just anybody, he expresses everybody's problems. The only thing that makes him different, as I have already mentioned earlier on, is his question.

Luke has seen so many people die by his hand that he came to wonder what happens in their head at the very moment they are about to die – and this becomes a question of the meaning of life. How does this question affect his behaviour?

He is focused on his question, he cannot prevent himself from asking it until he is obsessed by it, possessed by it, and it drives him further and further. He notices more and more things, and becomes more and more involved in the question. Luke (which sounds almost like 'look') always brings things too close – for instance he sets up this torture chamber for his WAPOS in his parents' house. When you are too close to things, you cannot avoid them, you have to cross them. He seeks the extreme – like his mother, but in the opposite direction – and takes the audience into the extreme situation. His is a very destructive journey, but it is also a journey of knowledge.

This is what drives him to perform this atrocity in the scene we mentioned earlier on: he had captured with his squad a woman with her baby in a forbidden no man's land. Because she is meant to be shot, Luke tries to force her to answer his question, and he starts a very vicious game that will end with killing the baby and her.

It is true Luke tortures his victims, but not to get some secret information of the sort torturers want, but to make them tell him the meaning of life. So in this scene it is important that the focus isn't on the violence – though it is indeed about killing a baby. Luke is not acting frantically out of cruelty or anger. He frequently asks what he can do next, he stops, makes silences and pauses and sometimes he changes direction. He wants to find out something and his process is very logical: he thinks that the only way he could get an answer is to put the question as close as possible to the Woman, to her or her baby's death. He treats them in a very practical way, like tools: a table and chair you can move. The point is to involve the audience in Luke's search, the quality of his questioning, how he constantly tries to define his question.

But he won't remain that cold and controlled and detached all the time. He ends by performing very strange acts with the baby.

Since nothing he tries works, he has to invent something new, he always has to proceed – and he makes the situation more and more extreme and *he* gets more and more involved in it until he becomes his own motive for doing this. It takes possession of him so that he moves to an extreme site where he acts differently. Luke reverts increasingly to childhood and its strange visions – because all children are visionary. He plays games as a child would: he says his jacket is 'Mr Jacket' and fools around with it, or holding the baby he runs against the wall of WAPO shields and then veers away from it. Playing games is always an attempt to elucidate the human situation by reducing it into a problem that is so small that you can grasp it in your hand. This 'Mr Jacket' performs every little act – the stages – of life until he dies. So the game is telling about the nature of time, the changes of seasons, of youth and age, and it sustains this tragic burden by a sort of comic-lyricism, or pathos. It is the knowledge hidden in Luke – he already knows what he is seeking, which is why he seeks it. In this sense, games are an extreme form of human behaviour – but they have no answers, only results – and in the end they are empty. That is why the winners are given medals and prizes, which is actually absurd – and totalitarian states worship sport. But eventually Luke's game with the jackets isn't extreme enough and he doesn't manage to get his answer from the Woman. So in the following scene, he plays at being the victim himself and tries to go to that moment when he is going to die in order to find out what life is about. But to know this he actually would have to die.

That is why in the last scene (to finally come back to it), he is brought back in the house among the people he killed and he can finally ask them directly the question.

It is as if the stone chasm of the previous scene had become the transparency through which he could see himself. Luke is always pushing the frontiers. He is like Odysseus who has to pass through hell to know if he will come back home. In the scene he finds himself in the situation of the neonate: he is so weak he has to be carried, fed and so on, and he can find food, heat and comfort only among the dead – so that he becomes like a foetus living in the womb of the dead. This is a journey allowed by the logic of imagination: it *recoups* reality, reminds reality of what it is, enacts its basis. His question eventually can awaken the dead – in my sleep imagery. It doesn't bring them back to life, obviously nothing can – and they can't give him a verbal answer. They keep silent and seem almost indifferent – because they are dead. Their sounds and movements are the opposite of WAPO 2's stamping. All they do is make a baby for Luke in which he knows what the answer already is. Luke is not the baby, he is the protector of the baby. The answer is that we are *born*, condemned, to be human. Looking for the meaning of life is like giving reality a name – but reality is called *Born*: you can't get away from being born. But this is immediately annihilated by Peter returning as a WAPO and turning the place into a concentration camp for the dead.

The play ends with a sudden return to the realism of the story line. The real WAPOS come back and shoot everybody, even the dead lying on the ground.

This shows in a straightforward way the WAPO organization of society as a prison submitted to the irrational with no way out. Donna can feed the dead forever, and the WAPOS can kill them over and over again. This is an everlasting concentration camp. Structurally, once the line of each character has been driven to its extreme, then the play has no further use for the world of imagination. The audience would know what is happening inside the characters and where they subjectively stand, so reality can come back again. The play had carried itself so far that it goes into a dream, to come back to what I have already said about sleep. Then it says to the audience: 'Know this dream the play is dreaming for you, so that you could be awake and know reality.' In this dream the play and the audience can explore profound imagery of the self, involving the nature of humanness and ultimately the creation of a just society. Drama is the interpretation of the community's dreams, its fictions. Its origin is the logic of imagination – that makes reality out of our fictions.

Anyway, practically, in the end the answer to Luke's question is never known.

No it isn't. It is not a solution to point to the ideal. The gesture would be more important than what is pointed at. Only Luke can answer Luke's question. When he has answered it – or taken the answer from what occurs, since he knows now that the answer lies in the baby that the dead made for him – he is silent. The end of the play leaves a huge question, but it has been clarified by Luke so that the audience can understand it. The point of the play is that after seeing it (properly staged) the audience can never stop asking the question. At the moment, at the end of the play, the answer would be the way the actor would hold the baby. That might be the Invisible Object.

What do you actually mean by that?

The Invisible Object is that part of the actor's performance that is unwritten in the text. It is something that drama extracts from the actor. An actor may make almost any incident in a play an Invisible Object, by choosing to use it to raise the moral and intellectual conflict at the play's centre. It is the profound confrontation of situation and humanness. It can be found in the usually ordinary, day-to-day world, in almost anything: a cup, a chair or a button, a word, a sound, a situation, an interchange with another – the actor himself, his movement, gesture, his handling of an object, anything that it is in his power to give. The soldiers on the top of the cliff in *Coffee* – to give you a practical example – load their guns professionally to shoot at people. But since on that day, as you remember, they have to aim and shoot their victims one by one, they can't do that as they usually do. So the way the actors would show how the soldiers are now, in this changed situation, loading their rifles – and one of them demonstrates great difficulties in changing his magazine – would be the Invisible Object. Any conventional act has in it this possibility, for example cutting bread – because both knives and bread have cultural meaning. In *Red, Black and Ignorant*, how the actress cuts the bread for her son who comes home after having killed his old neighbour could be the Invisible Object. Ideology made the object invisible and it can become visible again when the actor makes a new use of it and shows its human meaning in his performance. It may be that the character doesn't know the human meaning of killing, but the actor or actress would – and the Invisible Object could be the way he or she shows that the character *doesn't* understand and also the character's repression or ignorance and what these things cost him. The Invisible Object makes it possible to share with the audience the moral complexities of being human. The important point is that the audience are off their guard when they see a drama, and so they must see the Invisible Object – street ideology can't blank it out.

And from a practical point of view, in what way are your plays specifically helping to do this?

Only a play offers the occasion because the Invisible Object only exists on stage, among the actors – and it reflects into the audience's imagination. In describing my plays, as I am doing with you, I am only telling of the scaffolding, not of what is built on it. As a playwright I use every means so that the meaning doesn't flee from the place where it is, or hide somewhere else, but all that playwrights – and directors or designers as well – can do is to describe the site and the situations in which the Invisible Object is to be found. This is what my stage directions are ultimately about: they mean to lead the actor towards the Invisible Object, to point at the direction where he or she should go. Only the actor can enter this site, and *there* face choices only *he* or *she* has to decide – about how to use this situation, this event, this site and make the Invisible Object visible. The Invisible Object comes from the site so it really belongs to the self as it asks himself: 'What am I as a human being? What is the human logic behind what is going on?' It is almost primordial in humanness. It is the infant's recognition of the world as a home. This is why acting is the most important part of drama. Drama is really about acting and not writing.

So what does the actor have to do to make the Invisible Object visible?

He has to use the logic of his imagination. The Invisible Object can be analysed but it is above all an existential experience, a relationship the actor enacts. He does so not through stage images, but by committing his self, his being, to the enactment of his knowledge of the situation he is performing. It is not a matter of psychology of the character, it is the way the actor identifies his humanness and conveys this to the audience. This is the difference I make between acting and *enacting* – and the Invisible Object is the condition for enactment. Then imagination gathers together, integrates experience, meets with reason and together they create human meaning. It really is the ultimate meaning of the situation: it points at the site with all the social tensions, and the psychological tensions involved in them, at the structures, the paradoxes, the crises in real life, to which we are existentially connected. So everything an actor does is connected with the Invisible Object. In that sense it is the real motivation of people. It reveals the human dynamic in them – and thus it enacts reality. The true function of drama is to make the Invisible Object visible, without it drama is superficial. The Invisible Object is the most important thing we have to understand from drama.

How would the audience perceive it?

When an actor relates to the Invisible Object, audiences recognize themselves in it. It is the closest one subjectivity can enter into another's subjectivity. In this sense it can create a shared knowledge of what a shared humanness would be. For instance, the actor playing the bayoneted enemy in *Eleven Vests* could use his incomprehensible line in this foreign language as an Invisible Object. Then he won't be only saying to the Student: 'Why have you stabbed me?' – if that is what he says – but he would also be saying to the audience: 'Why are you watching this play?' It is a way of passing the responsibility to the audience. That is one of the uses of the Invisible Object.

9
NOBODY KNOWS HOW TO DEAL WITH INNOCENCE

Accident-time / The tin-can riot / *In the Company of Men*: a parricide prevented by a bird / Leonard needs to define what it is to be human in no man's land / Not even a thumbprint on the universe / Leonard versus Hammond / Alice inside the city / The *Pentad*: how to live a human life that is not a compromise with death? / From the crimes of the twentieth century to *The Crime of the 21st Century* / Sweden, the survivor par excellence / *Born, People* and *Innocence*: to accept the ontological responsibility of being human.

I suppose these small events, slips of ordinary, misplaced objects, unexpected acts, and so on, all these unusual details we have been pointing out and commenting on since the beginning of our talks, and which can so easily pass unnoticed, are like as many open invitations to actors to produce the Invisible Object.

Absolutely. These are opportunities to show what his or her action means to the character, as it appears to them *as* they perform it. It is as if the Invisible Object had to be seen from inside. In that sense, the scene in *Olly's Prison* I described earlier on, when Olly is mutilated and blinded, can turn everything on stage into an Invisible Object: his repeated phrase ('I can't see'), his movements, Frank's self-celebration, the apron over his uniform and, obviously, this act of fingering the dust and singing 'Dee-dum. Dee-dum'. Both characters are among the debris of an accident and Frank seems to see and understand all he usually doesn't, as if he was himself seeing the accident from inside within its own time.

How could Frank see better if he remains involved in the shock and the suddenness of an accident?

Well, this is a biological fact: you actually have such a feeling when you are involved in a real accident – as I experienced it myself years ago. I was driving (too fast) on a highway into London, when I suddenly lost control of my car and it went swerving in the middle of the traffic. Then, my mind started to work differently. Subjective time stretched and my observation became more complete: as I swerved in circles among the other cars, I noticed details I normally wouldn't, in particular a lorry driver – I noticed he was wearing a tie. He was angrily raising his fist at me, blaring his horn, I could see the lines and creases of panic on his face – and I thought of how pointless his reactions were. The cars were looking like whales, with huge heads and the rears tapering away like tails – because they were advancing towards me as I advanced laterally towards them and that modified the perspectives. I could even, calmly but regretfully, say to myself: 'Oh no, not like this' – and the tone of my voice in my head was lower than my normal speaking voice. I was also aware of the gap in time between *me-now* and when my car would seemingly collide with another car. It was a space of total silence surrounded by the noisy traffic, screeching tyres – which sounded to me like a mastodon's sigh – and the resonance of the blaring horn. So you see, you actually perceive the accident in a specific *clearer* way because you are involved in it – not like people seeing from the outside as something terrible or painful – or like the medics in the ambulance, with their job to do. You become conscious of the nature of movement, what is the movement relating to and so you are unexpectedly closer to the material world. It is as if time gains depth, so that you can observe the material connexions between things and make new ones. This is what I call 'accident-time' and this is actually how my characters see things when they are driven to their extreme and enter into the sort of monologues I have already talked about in *Jackets* or *A Window*, for instance.

NOBODY KNOWS HOW TO DEAL WITH INNOCENCE

What means do your plays provide so that such experiences can be reproduced and used on stage?

The point of accident-time is to combine alienation with intense involvement, as opposed to simply performing an incident or attending to it. The emphasis is on *time*, on the fact that something that seems fast can be seen slowly. (This is almost the opposite of slow motion in a film, which is aesthetic.) It allows another perception of the situation. It is an experience of clarity, of connecting, of seeing. In accident-time the unexpected catches your eye because it says: 'Look where you are.' Anything can produce accident-time, it doesn't have to be a frightful accident. Once I dropped a piece of quite valuable glass on a stone floor. It bounced and I was relieved because it didn't break at all – but it bounced so high that it fell again and broke. That was accident-time. In drama it occurs when the crisis reaches a climax so that the elements of the conflict can no longer be mediated. They irrupt in the situation and take it over. It is an inevitable chaos, but the situation reveals itself because the play's central moral dilemmas are now directly involved in it. For instance, remember the riot scene in *The Tin Can People*, in which the characters are destroying everything they possess. The danger of death has become unbearable and they can't live with it so that they are being taken over by the symptoms of their pathological fear. They become the victim of their own aggression. The play shows them in a state of frenzy, running out of control on stage but they all actually try to decipher the processes of what is happening to them at the moment they experience it.

They show this by carrying on, as the scene proceeds, separated and continuous monologues in spite of their frantic action. Are they speaking some sanity remaining hidden in them?

No, because, actually each one pursues a particular strand of madness to its logical end. One is homicidally berserk: she justifies everything by hate and supports this by attacking verbally and humiliating her victim. Another embodies universal nihilism: he sees through everything and everything seems meaningless and contemptible to him. A third one is so afraid of death she decides to pretend to be dead – and she tries to make it more convincing by movements demonstrating she can't move. And among those, two others are determined to defend sanity, though they show fear and desperation. So the actors of the scene have to be in different stage-worlds – which sometimes irrupt into each other – they have to be very much in control of what they do and what they mean in that situation and use the energy of the extreme they reach, but they don't enter into accident-time.

But you just said …

No: it is for the audience to be in accident-time. The scene puts them in such a position that they can see as if *they* were caught *themselves* in the accident: time is as if slowed, they have access to the different points of view involved, so that what would normally seem to be mere noises and rush appears as numerous and meaningful single details. Then chaos can show its cause. But accident-time really comes to the audience through their involvement in watching.

Nevertheless, one of your characters, Leonard in In the Company of Men, *describes something close to an accident-time experience. In the long speech in which he confesses to his father, Oldfield, that he tried to shoot him during a hunting party, Leonard tells everything he experienced as he was aiming through the sight, testifying to the density and the human complexity of that moment.*

Yes: Leonard is able to introspect and describe the process that went on in him – though it couldn't have lasted more than two seconds. His long description of the attempted murder demonstrates a new form of consciousness – as Hamlet does in his soliloquies. Then he finds a map of the universe inside himself. He is so concentrated on his decision to kill Oldfield that his mind is blotting out certain things and he attends to himself more carefully. He examines closer and closer what he sees and feels, and this brings him on a long journey through different worlds in which he looks at reality as a sort of totality where the dimensions of space and time just collapse and melt: he can see the world in its whole – he sees the sky itself grinning – as well as in close-up – he observes the pores of Oldfield's skin – or reverse its movement – he says the body attracts the bullet. He feels he can live every millionth of the seconds, fill them with eternity, and he can also see what is going

NOBODY KNOWS HOW TO DEAL WITH INNOCENCE

to happen the next minute, when he has fired the shot – which he will never do. He can even live Oldfield's time. He can *see* words, look at sounds.

And he doesn't shoot because in the middle of this fantastic vision, at the very moment he is ready to pull the trigger, he sees a bird through the sight of the rifle – and he will later say he stepped back because he didn't want to interrupt its singing by his shot.

Yes, but did he really hear the bird or did he only think he did? Anyway, something happened in his mind that made him hear the bird song and he then developed it into a map of the cosmos and human activities within it. And as he keeps going deeper and deeper into the universe and time, he enters into previously closed areas of his self and at the same time, into human raw material, and he meets even stranger images involving war, nails that become eyes and fingers crawling in the mud. It is as if he was standing at the edge of a cliff and only saw the sky – but by taking one more step towards the edge, he would then see an infinity of sea and sand down there – it changes everything but it can be seen only by coming right to the edge.

Why is this bird call so meaningful to him that it can make him renounce such a critical decision?

It is like in a Brothers Grimm tale: the bird tells him something about his situation that he hadn't realized, something like: 'Don't listen to me: listen to yourself. You have to ask yourself more questions. The point is not to get Oldfield's power. There is something beyond people's commitments or undertakings – or legal documents … And it won't be answered by killing Oldfield.' That puts him in a position close to Hamlet's when he is confronted with the supernatural world of ghosts: Leonard is asked the same questions. It is then as if the logic of the situation – Laius, Oedipus – which is that he should kill Oldfield, is opposed to the logic of Leonard, which is that he shouldn't. The singing is not sardonic, it is just a fact of existence – and it is very material: the bird sings in a real wood, not in some Garden of Eden. And remember this happens during a hunting party and everybody is there to kill the birds – but the bird sings … Actually the bird sings to anyone who bothers to hear it. Its song also sounds almost like a baby crying, so that when he points the gun at Oldfield's head he hears the sound of innocence.

When we attend to the scene as an audience, we see Leonard being stopped not by the bird, but by Bartley, who suddenly notices the gun is loaded and rips it from his hands. At that stage, everybody (audience included) thinks it is an accident – and Oldfield blames Bartley for it and sacks him on the spot, though he just saved his life. Later on Leonard will tell Bartley he was the one who prevented the murder, without mentioning the bird.

He doesn't practically, but he does on a deeper level. After he tells this, he re-enacts the scene imitating Oldfield and Bartley, to show how pointless it was, and he ends this by singing a song, 'The Camptown Races', which is about horses running round and round and round the tracks and not getting anywhere – a circular, pointless journey. The song is itself the meaning – could this be his translation of what the bird sang? Or is it that, having reached the bounds of experience, he can himself sing like the bird? Or maybe since his confession hasn't been heard – Bartley is then too drunk to hear it and just collapses unconscious – he can only sing?

The two versions of Leonard's incident can't go together. Why is the play presenting one factually for the audience to witness and contradicts it afterwards by the account of the character?

The first one cannot solve the problems. It prevented Leonard killing his father, but it doesn't explain why he wanted to do it or why he shouldn't. Leonard has experienced something for which he can't give the explanation you would expect: 'I hated him', or 'I was sorry for the stupid bastard but I had no alternative' – or the explanation a psychiatrist, or a police officer, or a fire alarm inspector would give. These belong to society and society only deals with the symptoms. But we have to *enter* the symptoms to get cured. We have to meet the tragic situation. In a West End play, we wouldn't structurally go beyond that first scene with the two armchairs and this glass of whisky I have already talked about: Oldfield would be coming in having won the war and, after he had been served a decent glass of whisky which he would have much appreciated, he would have been stabbed in the back by his allies and closest friends, joined ultimately by Leonard because he would be tempted by glory and power. Or in the scene when Leonard confesses Oldfield would have a heart attack because he is so shocked and this would lead anyhow to a reconciliation and everything would end happily after all. Oldfield might die but Leonard would inherit the company – and he would be sentimental enough to keep Bartley around. Everything would be solved and – that is the most important thing: *the business would be saved*. And the morality would be: 'How do I get to live by taking over the firm by ethical principles?' But my play in each scene says: 'No, that won't do.' There is not even Fortinbras to come at the end and restore the situation – or a chorus to assume responsibility for the play by stating: 'Don't call a man happy until he is dead and accept things as they are.' It tries on the contrary to demonstrate that we cannot carry on like that. The system won't be purified by getting rid of the villains – the Doddses or the Hammonds; we have to question reality more radically in order to decide how we should possibly live. The play is full of traps, conspiracies, treasons, deceits, but eventually the characters are always asking about telling the truth or being told the truth – as a contractual relationship between people. But the real question is: Who is the truth speaking to? Who is the bird singing to?

How is Leonard responding so that the play can carry out these questions?

He is searching for a role in life. He was found by Oldfield on the doorstep, where his mother, presumably, abandoned him. It abstracts him from the normal parameters of a child – family, parents, and so on – so that he doesn't know who he is and he has to find out for himself. But everything he tries turns against him. To begin with, he demonstrates a great desire for power and this is immediately used to manipulate him, by Dodds, into a conspiracy against Oldfield by Hammond, his rival. This is one of the reasons why he tries to kill his father: he sees it as a desperate way to disentangled himself from this trap. This makes him realize he cannot be one of these society's pirates in this the world of intrigue and subterfuge. So he decides to track down his real origins, that is to go back to the doorstep on which he is 'born' and see if he can find an answer there – if his true self has been left on the doorstep – if he can open the door and reprocess everything. Of course, when he gets there he finds that there is nothing left and he would never know anything about it. Then, he believes he has to be absolutely sincere, and he reveals to Oldfield the plot against him, and that he has been betrayed by his confidential agent, Dodds. By doing so, he repairs the situation and makes it work *and* he gets from his father power as a reward – the seat on the board he was asking for from the beginning. So Leonard seems to have sorted out the play – as teachers say: if you tell the truth it will be all right in the end. No, he hasn't, because, by revealing the truth about his situation, Leonard had weakened his old adoptive father so much that he collapses into a childlike impotency – as if he became the baby on the doorstep. So Leonard becomes responsible for him in a new human way and this is no more a matter of contracts and wills.

So, if I may sum this up: Leonard can't find out who he is because he only looks for himself inside the material, business world. But how can he go further?

Actually, what Leonard needs is a definition of what it is to be human and this cannot be found in his society, or the models and opportunities it provides. He is not seeking how *he* should live but how *people* should live – in the reality of drama, when a character defines his existence, he defines the existence of anybody because he has to make a decision for the whole of reality, or else he can't live for himself – what Antigone does is true to everybody. The characters in the play seem all to recognize this quality in Leonard to pose the problem of what is a human being and this enacts one of the basic contrasts of the play: the world of business, very determined, and the personal, imaginative, poetic experience of the characters. Everybody in the play is fascinated with Leonard and they all, at one moment or another, are tempted by Leonard into wanting, or needing, to be human. They all try, in their own way, to rescue him from his situation – as if by acting innocently towards him they could gain some of his innocence – and then they are driven to tell him the truth about themselves. But they don't think he listens. They all do this – except Dodds. Even Hammond, the worst of them, does.

NOBODY KNOWS HOW TO DEAL WITH INNOCENCE

Indeed it is very unexpected from the cynical manager Hammond is. He has even been searching for Leonard down in a derelict house when he was running away to look for his doorstep. There he reveals to him a terrifying plan for a global expansion of his food-processing business based on predation and the exploitation of war – he calls this strategy (after Hitler) 'butter and guns' because it means feeding and killing people at the same time. And then, suddenly, he offers to treat Leonard as his own son and to give him whatever he needs.

Yes, he pronounces it in a very long sentence – though his are usually quite short. His language becomes exploratory: he speaks like a blind man trying to read a map with his fingers, following the edge of Braille characters. It is as if he had never before said such a thing in his whole life. He tells Leonard he had opened a door that he normally keeps closed and he wants to enter that door by helping him. That is denying all the rules by which he lives. He desperately needs Leonard to tell him that he, Hammond, is not a monster. And then he doesn't know why he's saying these things. And as Leonard refuses he becomes merciless again: he threatens and eventually he does more than kill him, he says it will be as if Leonard was never born. It is this terrible thing of innocence. People want you to be corrupt because it is much easier to live with corrupt people. It is just a question of how much it will cost. But nobody knows how to deal with innocence. People are afraid of it.

If the others try – and fail – to find their humanness by confronting him, how could Leonard manage to get this definition of humanness?

He has to find out by himself. Human beings have no self-definition, no value *en-soi* – they can be reduced to corpses in death camps – neither can they get their value from things. They only have value by creating it themselves. Leonard doesn't need any other meaning for reality than the one he can create for himself. This means not only to define himself in his own terms, but in relationship to the universe. It is only in the extreme that he can define himself.

What is exactly this 'extreme' Leonard would have to go to?

As I have said about the Palermo Improvisation, in my plays I always define situations so that there is no escape – this means, no other solution, no other meaning than the one you create by yourself. It is always bringing the play, and the characters, and the audience, to the moment of decision. The characters have to reassess their situation and ask: 'What situation am I in? How am I in that situation?' – and ultimately: 'Who am I?' The questions become one. This is the process of being human. This is what the extreme is about. It is not a matter of horror, hysteria or Nietzsche's 'Live dangerously', but of total definition. All creativity is seeking definition of something in order to release reality. Once a character has reached the extreme he can see in the interior of himself and then explain himself. He can look back and understand all the journey of experiences he had to face to arrive here. The extreme situation contains *all* realities so the decision you make on that situation is total. Now, Leonard, in order to find himself, has to confront what Hammond called 'this little no man's land between father and son' – because his starting point is not the armchairs in Oldfield's drawing room but the doorstep where he was abandoned. This no man's land is the relationship he has to question more radically to find out who he is. Leonard has to understand that the confrontation with Oldfield is not a question of getting power in the business but of finding himself. Throughout the play the disputes between father and son send ripples round the world that allow him to question this. Leonard has to enter no man's land and to experience the extreme of this situation – no one can tell him what is there. There he can hear the bird. But it is not extreme enough – Leonard cannot just withdraw from the problem, he has to solve it. He has to go himself to where the bird is, become innocent as the bird, and this means to confess the truth to Oldfield, that he tried to kill him.

So, that was the reason for this long speech we began with. The funny thing is that, as Leonard tells him how he did not *kill him, Oldfield dies, without making a sign. So Leonard will never know if his father heard his confession.*

Yes: the father dies and the meaning of that can never be told – no doctor will write the reason for his death: listening to his son. Did the confession shake him? – So he was killed by the truth? – And not the crime? Or did he die naturally, before he heard a single word? Or

NOBODY KNOWS HOW TO DEAL WITH INNOCENCE

did he intend – satanically– to punish Leonard by preventing him ever knowing if he heard his confession? Or is it just an accident of life? – The stupidity of existence? However, this is the most destructive thing that could have happened to Leonard. He is left with his question and he takes on this very ambiguous situation. If Oldfield had left even a 'thumbprint' – says Leonard – which would demonstrate whether he heard or not, it would have meant that there is a meaning in the universe, that something moral could have even the slightest importance – or if somewhere in the universe there was a thumbprint that could be a mark of virtue or at least of honest human clumsiness – as a fingerprint is the indication of a crime. The universe is silent, thus empty, just like the big window at Leonard's back which went dark as he was confessing. There is nothing, nothing to tell him what to do, no guide in no man's land, no signpost – on which the bird could sit and sing. It is all meaningless. Leonard had to cross many barriers before he could tell the truth, and when he finally could, nobody was here to listen.

This is what he describes in his last long visionary speech to Bartley.

Yes. In it he sees his truth crossing the universe endlessly without anybody listening to it – as physicists say sounds cross the universe endlessly so that every event happens permanently. He unrolls a map of the universe and of time and of the human situation in it – as if he himself wishes to enter in every inch, every corner of the universe to experience its emptiness, its meaninglessness. So Leonard could never have a human relationship with the universe – just as if reality was playing tricks on him or the universe told him: 'I'm cleverer than you are. You don't know my secrets.' Leonard is lost in the middle of no man's land, the emptiness, and the meaninglessness, the no man's landness of reality. The doorstep is a thumbprint of nothingness in no man's land.

Is it because of this despair that Leonard ends up hanging himself in the scene immediately following?

Not at all. It is the same as with Shakespeare in *Bingo*. Seeing that there is no moral end in the world is the centre of tragedy. The tragic sense is the acknowledgement that reality is mad (as Lear finally says). Obviously, the determinants of reality could only be invented by a madman. So, why do I, a rational human being, have to live in this madness? But this is what enables you to face the extreme of madness and to bear that. That is what Hamlet means when he says: 'Readiness is all.' So, when Leonard (considering the lack of answers from his dead father) becomes conscious that this is a meaningless world and that he will never learn his identity from others, he realizes he needs to act to define himself – as if he became himself that person who picks him up on the doorstep. Then he could decide how he will use the universe, know what the universe wants to use him for.

So what does he do practically?

He has to perform an act that would define him in relationship to the universe. He decides to attack Hammond. Hammond is the really destructive modern force and Leonard sets him up, traps him, to confront him totally, that is with the terms of his whole life. His plan is to kill himself and use his suicide against Hammond. His gesture is evidence that 'butter and guns' (that is human kindness and the world of things) can never be reconciled for Hammond's profit. He knows it will hurt him because of his moment of innocence into which Leonard provoked him. Like Shakespeare he kills himself rather than contributing to this view, Hammond's view of the world.

And as he hangs he produces a gun and shoots at Hammond. He misses him but he frightens him so much that he can't sit on his chair any more – as you have already said – and before he leaves he kicks at the gun to be sure the ghost of dead Leonard won't come down from the rope to pick it up ... But Leonard also involves Bartley in his suicide: he pays him to kick the chair so that he hangs.

Leonard practically gives Bartley a new free life – he gives him a lot of money and his watch. Leonard saves Bartley because he is the person who has the vitality that is needed to survive this situation long enough to be able to understand its consequences and maybe to resolve it – because of his background of ordinary working-class people. He has the most to gain from change. He knows the world is a destructive place because he has been to the lowest levels – he says he has even served in a submarine designed to 'blow up the world'. He then discovers his innocence in helping Leonard to kill himself. I put my hope in him, because he has no illusion.

This is also what Alice does at the end of Chair: *when she realizes she has been discovered by authority and that Billy will be caught, she hangs herself but allows him to escape and spend one whole day in the real world he was eager to know. But she also asks him to scatter her ashes in a huge deserted car park so that the cars spread them in the whole city.*

Alice is a rebel. Her reality is controlled by that totalitarian power – I have already described it at length – but her imagination is not. She wants to deny she had ever existed to prevent that power from having control over her life and her death – she knows her acts and her suicide would be made to look uncontroversial. So she claims there is a part of her that they will never possess and that is a shared humanity. This comes from a true story: during the Chilean dictatorship, the regime wanted to erase totally the opponents it killed – among other reasons because some of their children were adopted by their torturers. So the police would scatter their ashes behind their cars for the traffic to spread them all over the city. In the play, Alice does it for the opposite purpose: more than disappearing, she wants her ashes to be everywhere, be smeared on the whole city, as if she was impregnating it with freedom, so that the city becomes her – in that simple sense. She then can say: 'I am too many for you to kill me. I am not me, I am everyone.'

Yes, but to do this she has to die – and she cannot prevent Billy eventually being shot. And Leonard may find himself, win a victory over Hammond, but however, at the end of the play, he still hangs dead. I see the human and moral point they are making, but, frankly, since they die anyway, *could this really be a satisfactory personal achievement?*

I don't think this is really the point because drama has to be *about* the audience. Leonard went to the extreme and so he took the audience somewhere they would not practically go. When they leave the play they should be saying not 'I'm going to hang myself like Leonard', but 'I'm going to pick up the baby'. In the same way Alice is really having her ashes scattered in the mind of the audience so that they would accept responsibility for her. This means she is warning them against their own government and reminds them that the price of freedom is vigilance. Drama goes to the extreme so that reality can become practical again for us. But actually, this is that part of the problem I tried to sort out years later with the Pentad: how would it be possible for Leonard to live without hanging himself? That is: living a human life that would not be a compromise with death. This comes to finding a *modus vivendi* between the world of values and the world of things and this can only be based on a human relationship with the world.

This 'Pentad' is your last series of plays to date consisting of Coffee, The Crime of the 21st Century, Born, People *and* Innocence. *You originally wrote them for Alain Françon and his actors who created the first three of them at the Théâtre national de la Colline in Paris. You elaborated it empirically, developing each play from the previous one, in the span of some fifteen years. What need did you have to carry on the same track for so long in so many plays?*

I didn't intend to, it came out of a necessity. Each play clarifies part of the problem and has its own victory and completeness – but answers always have a loophole where the question appears again. So I always had to write another play to return to the problem and it is only the overall cycle that can give a meaning to the events in all of the plays. For instance in *People*, the fourth one, I put a part of the problem aside, to secure another aspect of it. Then the characters, having understood the problem better, had to create a fifth play, *Innocence*, to confront in it the whole problem. So *People* exists in its own right – but it is also an overture for an opera which would be *Innocence*. It was always a reprocess or a re-examination. The question must *demand* an answer – that is what makes things radical.

The plays aren't connected by their story lines or characters, but, apart from Coffee, *which – as you explained earlier – refers to the Second World War, they are all set in the same future society – which is by the way the same as other plays you wrote in the same period, like* Chair, Have I None *or* The Under Room.

Coffee *deals* with the obviousness of the inhumanity of man, as it was exemplified by the past – I could have called the play *Europe 41*. I was asking: 'Why did it happen?' Then, after looking at the crimes of the twentieth century the question arose of the crime of the next century. And this 'crime of the twenty-first century' is really Primo Levi's 'Here is no why': to withdraw the question 'why' and put in its place a mechanical and atavistic explanation for inhumanness – the world of things, that there is no freedom based on imagination and the rational only produces coercion and social ghettos. So I projected the 'Fourth House' of *Coffee* a hundred years ahead, when the soldiers on the top of the cliff have become the force of government. But this is really about the present because I intended to point to what is happening now but is invisible. We cannot easily know, cannot rationally calculate, what our present social troubles and violence will turn into in the future – just as people inventing the motor car couldn't foresee our traffic problems. Problems grow unseen, inch by inch, until it is too late to go back and what was unthinkable becomes inevitable. The impossible always occurs in history. Could we have conceived Auschwitz in 1900? Hitler set about his intentions as soon as he got power, but that was an area people didn't visit when they voted for him. They thought that he would make the trains arrive on time – but they didn't know the trains would go to Auschwitz. On the gate of hell isn't written 'Those who come here, lose every hope' but 'Welcome to the Promised Land'. And people go in with joy, making festivals. Tears only come later. These plays show the future to which what is happening now is leading us. That is why in *Born* I show this destruction of society taking place in a very recognizable social context with Peter and Donna and their baby just moving into a new house – as you remember. The future might seem bright but their society is not in control of itself and the play follows out the logic and shows it collapsing.

And, indeed, we saw that, by the time their baby was a grown-up adult, they are being ruled by the WAPOS and deported.

Just as German society collapsed between 1918 to 1939. Things can actually change much more rapidly than you would think possible and society *can* degenerate in such a situation that we are not in control of what we are doing. But the point of the Pentad is not only to observe the destruction of the society, but to examine the process that enables this inside the human mind. It is only when you can understand the origins of humanness that you can have any chance of understanding the problem. I pursue the problem not through theory – because to *be* right in the human situation is not the same as to *make* it right – this is why revolutions go wrong – but through the lives of individuals, and this implies making the character transparent to himself or herself.

You achieved this by resorting to these various interventions of imagination we discussed earlier on about Coffee *and* Born.

I realized this only later, but all the plays of the Pentad are digging, unfolding, exploring this scene in the forest in *Coffee*. Everything was there, but it needed to be opened, explained, developed. In each play I re-examine this core relationship (that is what Greek drama is also about), which lays down the foundations of the mind and puts the characters in the most radical position. I put them in various sites but also always into different relationships with the objective world because your own reality doesn't end at the end of your fingertips. *Born* begins by observing them in a social context – then in the last part I push the play back to the foundation of human beings. It is the same in *Innocence*: the play is absolutely set in reality but at the end the main character, the Son, just like Luke goes back into the world of the neonate. But he goes one step further and is confronted by the creation of the tragic in the human mind. Whereas in *The Crime of the 21st Century* I keep these core relationships on this site resembling a human body within its boundary, as in a bowl, where I could isolate them and examine with them as society within the self – it is like putting a camera inside a head. It is the same with *People,* but it concentrates not on the pressures of society on the individual but on how the individual processes his relationship to reality. Then *Innocence* relates the two sides of the coin, the two aspects of the self and works out these relationships. All this constitutes an attempt to design a pattern for human living, a role for human beings in the modern world. The question of the Pentad is: 'What does it mean to be human?' It is exactly the opposite question of: 'Will Godot come?'

How is this question articulated and carried over throughout the plays?

At the end of *Coffee*, Nold claims he 'survived' – and it is true: he came out of the pit of Babi Yar alive and his innocence has not been corrupted by his experience. He says so with his eyes, fists and jaws clenched – he knows what it costs: it is written in his own darkness. This could be an answer to the problem of the coffee cup but it won't solve all his dilemmas. These would need to be looked at more closely to be sorted out. *The Crime of the 21st Century* intends to show this cost of being human, that it costs you something to survive in our society – and it will destroy all the characters of the play. Each one is resistant to this crushing authority and is conscious that he or she needs to be human. It imposes on them as a necessity, as if they had taken an oath on themselves. They can be violent to each other, but it is always on a moral ground – to save someone else and make a new, valuable life. They all have a story about the moment they realized this need and left their nightmarish society to flee to this desert part of the world: one, Grig, decided to escape from his wife who was dying of a cancer; another one, Grace, left everything because she discovered she has been lied to about her origins and needed to confront her real mother; and the main character, Sweden, because he didn't want to die among the zombies in the Prison-city.

Sweden is a young hooligan and arsonist, a rebel, always on the run, full of vividness and desire to live, Jack-the-Lad, but also capable of great violence.

After Nold, Sweden is the survivor par excellence: he would do everything to stay alive. He represents the structural urgency of freedom. It can be buried or corrupt, but its potential remains always there. He has no place to be free but he is his own freedom. He accomplished this spectacular walk away from prison across the desert – the play uses the imagery of walking to expose the character's will for freedom. He ends blinded, with his hands bleeding and he literally has no feet – he can't count his legs to say if he is human as Oedipus did in answer to the Sphinx. This expresses our modern condition.

This is a terrifying image: Sweden is caught twice by the army as he is on the run. The first time, the soldiers force him into gouging his own eyes out, the second time they cut off his feet and leave him by himself in the wilderness.

But even when he is blinded he could still walk alone in the desert and with no feet he can still 'dance' on his stumps, exert his human energy against the violent inertia of the world – and eventually he literally *crawls* away. Sweden suffers because of his wounds but he talks only about his humiliation, the moral, the *human* pain. He loses his autonomy, his human ability to decide for himself. This is what the authority wanted to mutilate in him – so that he couldn't dance any more and his 'why' would become powerless. He had to submit to what the soldiers demanded and committed an atrocity against himself. He could never escape from this – as he did from the prison: the army has won. His mutilation is authority's trade mark, the irrevocable mark of chains on the mind. The soldiers blinded him without any logic or military motive – they didn't even laugh, which could at least have shown that they knew what they were doing, as a last token of humanity, though depraved.

He says as a pathetic comment to himself: 'That's what we are now.'

Sweden is ashamed of them, ashamed of them for being human. It is the ultimate deprivation of his right, his need, to be human, to be oneself. He is absolutely in the power of his captors, he is taken away from himself. His existential journey is not only physical – his obvious mutilations – or psychological – his murders or unexpected gestures – it is also an active meditation on humanness. I called him Sweden as a reference to Hamlet.

You aren't saying this seriously, are you?

Well, I couldn't call him 'Dan Mark', could I? Sweden is a Lear who has the age of Hamlet, if you want. Everything he does after he has been blinded is an assertion, a restoration, of his right to be human. He fights for this and pins everything on it. But he does it in a way that is not humanly acceptable and his actions are of course disastrous for the other people involved. This would never build a community.

NOBODY KNOWS HOW TO DEAL WITH INNOCENCE

Indeed: he actually stabs to death, with great violence, two women, first Hoxton, who fostered him, and then her daughter Grace, though he was in love with her and wanted to go away with her.

Even when his acts are inhuman, his motives aren't. Sweden didn't come here to kill people. He is forced by his situation of being reduced to a powerless infant in that wilderness. If he could see, and therefore look after himself, he would never have killed the women. He kills them because they put him in danger of returning into the control of the soldiers, the ultimate dehumanizers. He has escaped from prison, as if from hell, and the logic of this choice is to escape from the bad world – this is his human imperative. He still is driven by the terror he is escaping from and everything that stands in his way is an abstraction that he would remove. It is like the madness sent by the gods to Ajax that makes him slaughter the sheep instead of his enemies, or that makes Hercules kill his children. He kills Hoxton because she won't help him or give him a reason to live. She cannot make him feel like a human being – she doesn't even *say* something which would make him endure this with humanness or free him from the inhumanness. When he kills Grace, he says: 'Tell me it's wrong! Wrong!' There is despair, but there can never be submission. At the end he will not submit even to the help Grig offers.

He then also harshly refuses to be a human being any more and he leaves to join the stray dogs populating the ruined wilderness.

He can't endure being human any more: the burden of it is too big for him. This is too demanding, too wounding. It cost him too much. It is as in the *Oresteia*, this moment I found marvellous when Electra goes to her father's tombstone and says: 'I cannot do this'. She doesn't put herself behind a banner, she is more human: she shows what it costs her. But only a human being can have such a thought, can mean such a value. This is when Sweden is the most human. No dog – or rat– could say: 'I don't want to be a dog' – or a rat. It is very human of him because he knows the cost of being human and still he insists on demanding humanness, even if he can reach it only by living with dogs. The play states that this is the infernal, intolerable mess you make of being human (and the last century was appalling) but you cannot escape *ever* from the responsibility of being human – and you can't let God or Stalin discount that cost for you.

The next play is Born, *with Luke and his question we have already discussed at length. We also said that he didn't obtain an answer to it. Nevertheless how does his radical questioning contribute to the proceeding in the cycle of the general question about what it means to be human?*

Luke is not the only one: the other characters come to their own conclusions about his question from their experience in the play. You remember that Donna nurses the dead because she cannot bear that there is suffering in the world? She thinks that in order to be human she must extend herself to the others, dedicate herself to their pain, be responsible for them and give her humanity to them. Peter's answer is: 'If we understand some a' what we do we got a right t' live.' A part of the cost of being human, of recognizing your humanness, means to become conscious of what you have done, as Nold or the characters of *The Crime of the 21st Century* have experienced it. But Luke needs to go one stage further. It is not enough to be human, you have to accept responsibility for being human – only then you have the possibility to create a human society. Luke can't verbalize the extremity – he can only howl, like Grig in his grey room at the end of *The Crime of the 21st Century*. This is the tragic pain at the human condition, the ontological responsibility of being human. Luke is asking what the meaning of life is as such, as a general question. But, in the end there is no answer to Leibniz's question: 'Why is there anything rather that nothing?' Then your question has to be: 'Given that situation what do I do in it?' So to go further I needed characters who ask what is the meaning of their life in their actions.

This is People, *the fourth play. It is a strange compact network of four characters meeting on the same site on which one of them is dying. They were all members of different murderous troops – except one woman, Lambeth, who is marauding in mass graves and battlefields – and they all have difficulties with a past story they can't sort out – one is amnesiac, another one keeps repeating it continuously, another one keeps it secret.*

They are fighting to find out what happened to them in order to take their particular responsibility for it. It is like a summing up speech in a trial where various lawyers are giving their version of what happened. For instance, the amnesiac – I call him Someone – since he doesn't remember his story, he has to find the reality of his past in order to have his self – and for different motives he believes the other characters may know him. When he discovers who he is, he accepts the fullness of being human. (He doesn't say: 'So, I am the world-famous concert pianist!')

He does when he hears another story, Lambeth's. She tells how when she was caught by the army with her two boys, the soldiers told her to choose to save one of them – and obviously they shot this one. Why does it have this revealing effect on Someone?

Because he understands from her story that some situations are beyond your control but it won't stop you acting – everybody has their own freedom and responsibility and they make out of their life what they can. Lambeth's choice turned out not to have the effect she wanted, but she chose it in good faith. It is the first time she tells this story and it is as if she was giving something to Someone. He then can accept his situation, without lying to himself any more about what he did or blaming himself for it. On the other hand, the dying man, Postern, knows what happened to him: he was a killer in a squad and was shot by his fellow troopers. But it is essential for him to believe in the possibility of innocence because he then could assume that he did what he did, not because he was evil but because he had lost his innocence. This would humanize the world for him and make him more human. He cannot bear to have lived in a world in which there was no innocence. But this means he doesn't want to understand himself. He just wants somebody else to do it for him and when he recognizes innocence in Someone's face and behaviour, he wants him to be his innocence – like Christ, or like Hammond with Leonard. So he insists on proving that Someone has never killed anyone. This is a naïve idea of innocence as something untouched by reality – whereas innocence is knowledge at the end of the universe and no one can go there for you. Postern can believe this because his own reality is severed from innocence. He is eventually destroyed by Someone's insistence on his own culpability. At the end of the play, once Lambeth and Someone have found the strength to face the problem and established who they are, they can leave the site to journey back into the world. So the next play, *Innocence,* will enact their experiences within the problems of social reality.

This last play is very long and seems to call all the figures, types of characters, signs, objects, sites, imagery, situations, relationships, everything that participated in the other plays and sets them down to work together again. How does the play conclude the cycle?

In the end, the Son is loaded with the experiences and resolutions of the previous characters of the four previous plays – Nold, Sweden, Luke and Donna … He combines their knowledge in a new synthesis which is his own and produces the central speech of the Pentad: 'I have an ache carved in my body. I want to be human. That is why I fight. Myself and anybody else. If I didn't there'd never be peace anywhere.' He doesn't die like Hamlet or find a peaceful resolution like Prospero. He has to *struggle*. That justifies understanding and redeems action. He recognizes there is no release from the responsibility of being human – and you can only become yourself by making the problem your own, knowing that the responsibility for the problem finally comes down to *you. You* have to confront it in the world and that means to accept the responsibility for the world. This is what I understand as *the human imperative* and this is where our innocence lies. This is what all the characters of the Pentad are enunciating at the end of their plays – and Leonard too when he made his decision: you are responsible not just for your life, or for what happens on your doorstep, but for the universe. You have an extreme moral responsibility.

EPILOGUE:
THE STAGE IS *US*

The human imperative / *Existence*: an x becomes a person / Why drama is necessary.

I won't try to sum up our talks, but it seems that this 'human imperative' we eventually came to is the basic dynamic of drama as you understand it.

It really is. But it is important that its origins are understood. It is not given to us by the world, *we* give it to the world. Everything inside the play – space, time, metaphors, actions – is there to settle the human imperative as a necessity. My plays create extreme situations in which the grip of ideology on the self is broken so that imagination has to be brought to the surface to respond to it. This enacts a new scene inside reality in which a solution can only come from the imperative to humanness. That is what tragedy is about. It has nothing to do with submission to fate, it doesn't purge the audience of anything. The horrors we see when we watch a tragedy matter because we are conscious they happen in the human situation. Tragedy is the recognition of the responsibility of being human, therefore of your responsibility for the world. We have to understand what is our relationship to our site and how we create it. This is a political and social question. This is what I am interested in and in that sense I am joining together the Greek and the Jacobean theatres – the Greeks' obsession with the meaning of reality and the gods and Shakespeare's obsession with the individual. It is not a matter any more of a curse or gods saying: 'This is right and this is wrong' – nor of individuals asking: 'What is happening in me?' – it is asking the audience: 'Who are you on this site, for which you are responsible?' The purpose of drama is to remind the audience of their innocence by showing them it – like something you already know but tried to forget. We are not responsible for your crimes but for our innocence. Until we understand this we will commit crimes.

How do you mean an audience to be practically part of such a process?

I alter the directions *for them* so that they are lost and have to find new ways of understanding. Their *understanding*: that's what I am questioning. This would mean putting them in the position of the chorus in the structure of Greek drama – which monitors the play and maintains its relationship with the protagonists with comments and questions like: 'Where are we now? What do we think of this now? What is the meaning of this?' The point about drama is not to avoid the problem, or find tricks to solve it, but to meet the problem straight on and explore it as far as you can. This is the point of this exercise I designed for actors where I ask them to move a chair closer to a table but without touching either of them. There is no solution to it, the point is to face the problem and understand it. When people know they have a problem, then you have drama – and nowadays, we don't only have problems but disasters. When they are involved in the situation in accident-time, audiences will seek the meaning of what they see and since it is drama it engages in certain structures in the mind involving their profoundest moral and human awareness. The play then takes place in their lives and not just in their role as spectators. Because a play is a drama, not a lecture or an admonition: it is an enactment of total reality.

What difference does what you call 'enactment' make to, say, an exposure or a representation or even a performance of reality?

Drama analyses the question on an ontological level, not only on a social or political level. A very last straightforward example of this could be this short play I wrote for the radio, called *Existence*. It deals with a young burglar who breaks into a house looking for money – and he ends by looking for himself. The burglar is called x. It has to be a small x, not a capital, the minimal indication of somebody, because he doesn't know himself. So the play speaks about an 'x' that turns into a person. If I was into typography then in the printed text I would

EPILOGUE: THE STAGE IS *US*

make the x larger and larger throughout the play. Almost the whole play takes place at night in a totally dark room. It only begins to get some light at the end. In the dark x falls over somebody else in the room. I called him Tom. He and x seem to be the only people in the house. x tries to force money from him. As with Luke and Mike and some of the other characters we've talked about, x doesn't get an answer to his questions and so they become bigger. Tom just keeps repeating the same incoherent noise. Almost an animal sound. As x insists he broadens his questions more and more. He becomes obsessed with Tom. Why was he sitting there on his own in the dark? Why wasn't he asleep? Why doesn't he speak? Why why why? – and then x starts talking about himself and his life, and so on. When the situation gets out of hand, he begins to ask why he should ask a question – even if he was given an answer what would that mean? His mind begins to be creative and he creates his own extreme. But the point I wanted to make here is that he is not thinking of it in that way. He is *experiencing* thought.

What do you mean by that?

He doesn't say: 'This is what I mean. This is what I think.' He *does* something that enacts it. For instance, at one moment he tries to get away from *this place* – because he feels it is dangerous – but he immediately comes back because he understands there is no point in returning back to street-reality if he refuses this confrontation – he would never be free, he will always bring this place with him. But what he does is he runs down, jumps down the steps, then he walks back up and barricades himself inside the room – it is equivalent to the frantic movement of his thought. In the beginning he breaks things in the flat both to threaten Tom and to try to find the money by himself. Since he doesn't get an answer, he goes on until the flat is entirely devastated. This enacts both asking the question and getting no answer. The questioning and the destroying go together and make an experience of drama. This ends when there is just one cup left in the kitchen – and he still has no answer – so the universe is in this cup. After all that chaos and these strange sounds of destruction, there is silence – and then one cup breaking – the universe breaking.

He eventually discovers why Tom doesn't answer when (still in the dark) he puts his hand in his mouth: he has no tongue – he must have been mutilated in some way.

Then he is like Dante descending through the Inferno. x literally says: 'What 'appens in this room? What's it for? It's 'ell!' He is faced with the ultimate horror – he knows he will never have an answer. The text just says: 'Flat. Terror.' It points at an experience of terror so complete that you become it totally. x has reached a state so extreme it is far beyond normal human experience – and he is lost there. It is as if he were living totally – as opposed to the fact that your life (or your death) is in a way something *done* to you. x is not terrified by something done to him, he is at a stage further: he has become the terror. Here all ideas collapse and there is no language to say it – because language can only say the opposite.

Is that why at the end, x desperately tries to prevent Tom from writing on the wall?

Yes: he knows it will be used as an explanation of what is happening in that room – by judges or policemen – and any interpretation by anybody outside the room would be wrong. Language couldn't contain this experience: the words won't have the meaning of the sentence in the room. These are the situations in which drama becomes necessary – because it uses language to say something philosophy can't. In this sense, the play really enacts the structure of the nature of drama – in this structure Oedipus, Antigone, Lear take place. It doesn't use drama to tell a story: it is the story telling itself to itself in order to analyse drama. This is the extreme my plays intend to go to – as Dante had to go to hell. But Dante was guided by a classical poet and divided the universe into spheres – hell, purgatory and paradise. If you are to visit hell now, you need not Virgil but Aeschylus and Euripides – and you can't divide space as Dante did: you have to make hell a human space. At the end the only means x has to prove that he is alive is to enact the imperative to be human: life is of supreme importance but our society is now so empty that it has no other means to respect – honour – this truth – this imperative – than by killing: x forces Tom to shoot him. It is the only way he can live in the culture in which we now live.

EPILOGUE: THE STAGE IS *US*

This is the experience of the character. How does this relate to the audience?

In drama you are confronted with a situation for which you have to do something, and since it is happening in your head, you are involved and responsible for it because the scene on the stage *is* the scene in the mind – you can't merely observe it as in poetry. The audience has to choose, to make their decision in the conflict on the stage. They ask: 'What should I do in that situation?' which comes down to: 'Who am I?' – because you are involved in asking the question to *yourself*. In this sense, when my characters go on their journey in order to find themselves and create their humanness, they take the audience with them. The actor signals back to the audience who they are. If they can follow it, then it is a journey towards their humanness. It might be only one step or a shuffle forward, but as long as it is in the right direction it is an experience of freedom – and that experience is always a leap. Drama is not somebody telling you who you are or should be. It demands that you define yourself with your decision. It has to be absolutely unavoidable. These are moments when you meet yourself – which in real life people may avoid doing. This is what drama requires of you. Normally an audience is expected to sit there and watch something in order to make a judgement about it – hopefully with impartiality. Drama doesn't ask you for an alienated judgement, because it deals with nobody else's case but yours. It is as if you were watching some Agatha Christie murder mystery: the inspector is moving closer and closer to the solution, then he comes down the stage, walks into the audience, reaches your seat and says: 'The murderer is you.' That's why Brecht is wrong. Brecht sees the chorus as the real society, the community – so he reduces the play to the chorus. This is what he should do – but he does not see that everyone in the chorus is Oedipus, Antigone, Hecuba, Medea. He ends with an abstraction – and a human abstraction is a prison. The stage is us, not an abstract calculation. Then you can accept responsibility for yourself and the world. When this is sorted out it is a basis for a democratic relationship to the world – and democracy is not other people: it is *you*.